The First Dynasty of ISLAM

The Umayyad Caliphate AD 661–750

G. R. HAWTING

SOUTHERN ILLINOIS UNIVERSITY PRESS
Carbondale and Edwardsville

Published in Great Britain by Croom Helm Ltd., Provident House,
Burrell Row, Beckenham, Kent BR3 1AT
Published in the United States and Canada by Southern Illinois
University Press, P.O. Box 3697, Carbondale, IL 62902-3697

Library of Congress Cataloging-in-Publication Data

Hawting, G. R. (Gerald R.), 1944–
    The first dynasty of Islam.

    Bibliography: p.
    Includes index.
    1. Islamic Empire—History—661–750. I. Title.
DS38.5.H39 1986   909'.097671   86-6473
ISBN 0-8093-1324-3

Contents

v

Conventions

Dates Unless there is a particular reason for providing the Islamic, *hijri* date, all dates are AD.

References In the notes to the text, given at the end of each chapter, references are usually to the name of the author or editor and a short form of the title of the work. Full titles, together with date and place of publication, are provided in the bibliography. See the list of abbreviations for the titles of journals, etc.

Transliteration A full scholarly transliteration is not provided in the text but the bibliography and index are transliterated. The bibliography reproduces the various methods of transliteration used by the authors cited. My transliteration follows the system of the *Encyclopaedia of Islam*, with the few modifications customary in works in English. On the whole, readers without any Arabic will safely ignore the transliteration symbols, but may wish to note the following:

' = the Arabic letter *'ayn*, a guttural sound produced by constricting the larynx;

' = the *hamza*, a glottal stop like the *tt* in the Cockney pronunciation of *butter*;

vowels are short unless they have a macron (¯) over them;

ibn (abbreviated to b. in the middle of a name) = 'son of';

B. (abbreviation of *Banu*) = 'descendants of', 'family of', 'clan of', 'tribe of', as appropriate.

Abbreviations

AIEOr.	*Annales de l'Institut des Études Orientales*
AIUON	*Annali, Istituto Universitario Orientale di Napoli*
AJSL	*American Journal for Semitic Languages and Literatures*
BSOAS	*Bulletin of the School of Oriental and African Studies*
BZ	*Byzantinische Zeitschrift*
CMedH	*Cambridge Mediaeval History*
EI1	*Encyclopaedia of Islam*, 1st edition
EI2	*Encyclopaedia of Islam*, 2nd edition
GS	I. Goldziher, *Gesammelte Schriften*
IC	*Islamic Culture*
IJMES	*International Journal of Middle East Studies*
IOS	*Israel Oriental Studies*
IQ	*Islamic Quarterly*
Isl.	*Der Islam*
JA	*Journal Asiatique*
JAOS	*Journal of the American Oriental Society*
JESHO	*Journal of the Economic and Social History of the Orient*
JRAS	*Journal of the Royal Asiatic Society*
JSAI	*Jerusalem Studies in Arabic and Islam*
JSS	*Journal of Semitic Studies*
MW	*Muslim World*
PPHS	*Proceedings of the Pakistan Historical Society*

Rend. Linc. Rendiconti dell Accademia Nazionale dei Lincei,
            Classe di scienze morali, storiche e filologiche
RH   Revue Historique
RHR   Revue de l'Histoire des Religions
RO   Rocznik orientalistyczny
RSO   Rivista degli studi orientali

SI   Studia Islamica

WI   Die Welt des Islams

ZA   Zeitschrift für Assyriologie
ZDMG   Zeitschrift der deutschen morgenländischen Gesellschaft

Glossary*

amīr	'commander'; an army leader and/or governor of a province
amīr al-mu'minīn	'Commander of the Believers'; a title of the caliph
ashrāf	leading members of the leading families among the Arab tribesmen
barīd	the system of communications between the provinces and the caliphal court
bay'a	the pledge of allegiance given to a caliph, heir apparent, or contender for power
dār al-islām	the regions under Muslim government in contrast to the **dār al-ḥarb** ('house of war')
da'wa	'call', 'propaganda'; the movement which prepared the way for the 'Abbāsid takeover of the caliphate
dīnār	the gold coin
dirham	the silver coin
dīwān	the register of individuals entitled to pay or pension from the government; a government department
fils	the copper coin
fiqh	the theory of Islamic law (not the law itself, the *sharī'a*)
fitna	conflict within the Muslim community, especially that between 'Alī and Mu'āwiya
ḥajj	the pilgrimage to Mecca in the month of Dhu'l-Ḥijja

xi

imām	a) the supreme head of the Muslims, particularly used in this sense by the Shī'ites b) a prayer leader in a mosque c) an honorific title applied to a religious scholar
jizya	a tax, in the classical system a poll tax (tax on individual persons)
jund	'army'; a military district
khalīfa	'deputy'; the caliph
kharāj	a tax, in the classical system a land tax
khuṭba	a speech; in the early period any speech of importance delivered by a figure of authority, especially the caliph or governor; eventually developing into the sermon delivered at the mid-day prayer service in the mosque on Fridays
majūs	'Magian'; in the strict sense Zoroastrians but used more widely for followers of religions other than Judaism or Christianity to whom the Muslims wished to grant some toleration
mawlā	'client'; a non-Arab who has accepted Islam; a follower of an important individual
ṣalāt	the ritual, five times daily, prayer service of Islam
shurṭa	a small force used by the governor or other authority to keep order
sunna	'accepted usage or practice'; eventually identified with the *Sunna* of the Prophet, the usage of Muhammad which Sunnī Islam accepted as being, together with the Koran, the main source of authority for its law
'ulamā'	the religious scholars of Islam
wali'l-'ahd	the heir apparent

* The meanings given are those usually applicable in this book. In other contexts the words may have other meanings.

Figure 1: The 'Northerners'

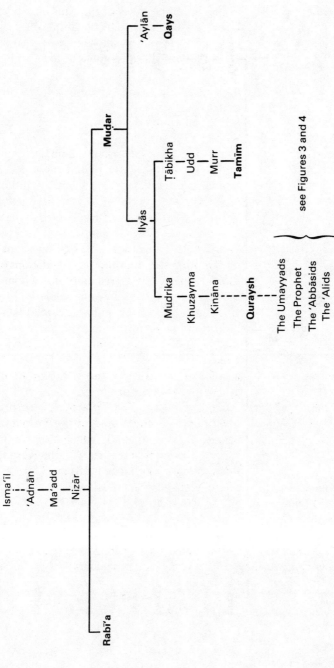

Isma'īl
'Adnān
Ma'add
Nizār

Rabī'a

Muḍar

'Aylān
Qays

Ilyās

Ṭābikha
Udd
Murr
Tamīm

Mudrika
Khuzayma
Kināna
Quraysh

The Umayyads
The Prophet
The 'Abbāsids
The 'Alids

see Figures 3 and 4

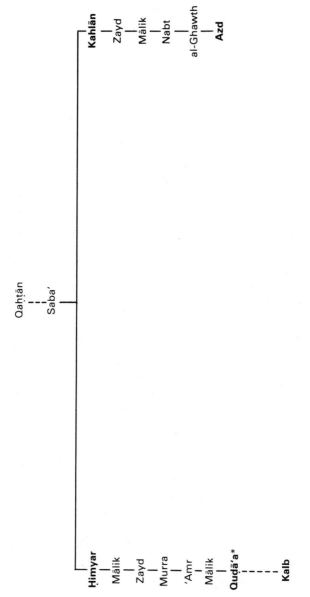

Figure 2: The 'Southerners'

Qaḥṭān
|
Saba'

Himyar
|
Mālik
|
Zayd
|
Murra
|
'Amr
|
Mālik
|
Quḍā'a*
|
Kalb

Kahlān
|
Zayd
|
Mālik
|
Nabt
|
al-Ghawth
|
Azd

* This is the 'revised' version of the genealogy of Quḍā'a — see p. 36.

Figure 3: The Umayyads

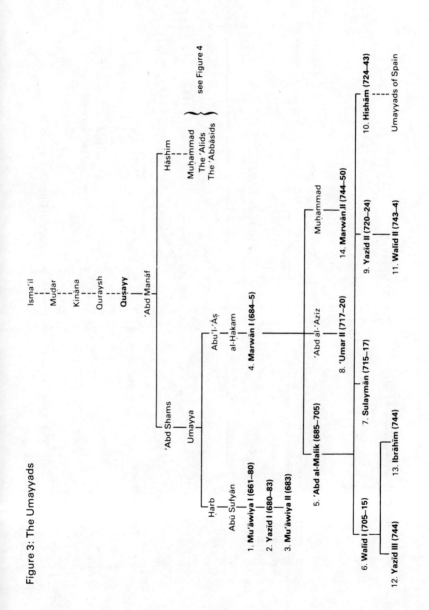

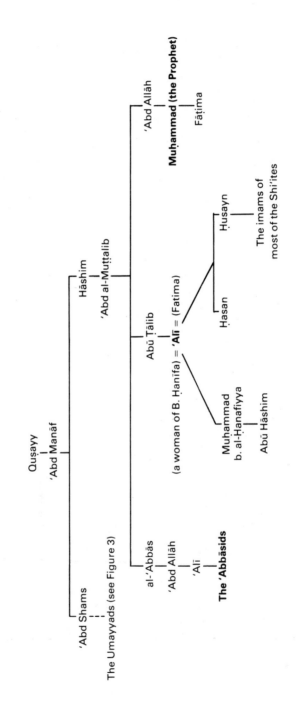

Figure 4: The Other Descendants of 'Abd Manāf

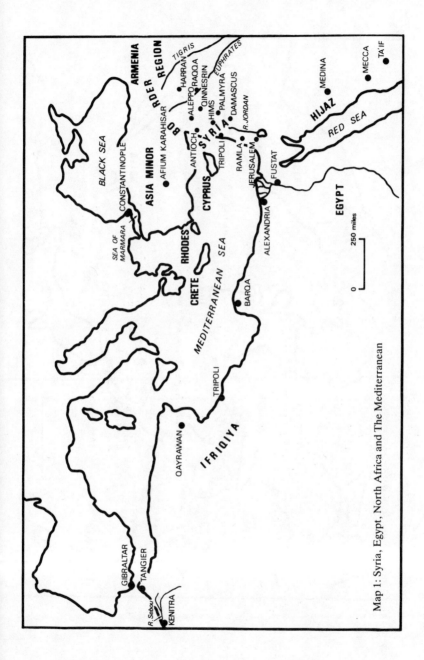

Map 1: Syria, Egypt, North Africa and The Mediterranean

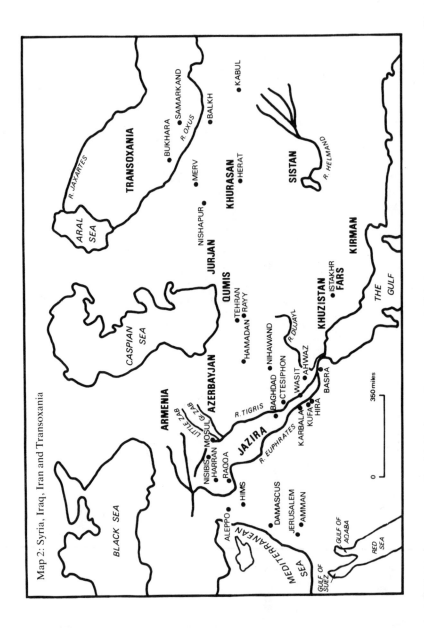

Map 2: Syria, Iraq, Iran and Transoxania

Preface and Acknowledgements

Between the general surveys of Islamic, Arab or Middle Eastern history, of which there are several of varying quality, and detailed monographs on particular aspects of Umayyad history, many of which are not in English, there is little that can be recommended confidently as an introduction to the importance, main events and personalities, and problems of the Umayyad period. The present work tries to provide such an introduction.

The standard modern account of Umayyad history is Julius Wellhausen's *The Arab kingdom and its fall*, first published in German in 1902 and translated into English in 1927. In spite of the inevitable dating of Wellhausen's own political and religious outlook, and the criticisms of his method of source analysis made recently by Albrecht Noth, his book remains of fundamental importance for anyone wanting more than an introductory knowledge of Umayyad history, particularly its political and military events. The present work is certainly not intended to supersede *The Arab kingdom*.

As an introduction, however, experience has shown that Wellhausen's work is not especially suitable. Leaving aside the rather idiosyncratic English of its translation, it contains more detail than is readily absorbed, its presentation is not as clear as modern readers expect, and its concern with source criticism is not appreciated by those who do not have even a simplified traditional narrative against which to set it. Attempts to get students to read and digest Wellhausen usually result in puzzlement and the beginnings of a conviction that Umayyad history is too difficult for undergraduate study.

But there is really little else, especially in English, which treats the period as a whole and which can serve as an introduction. M. A. Shaban's first volume of his *Islamic history. A new interpretation*, it is true, is readily available and does provide a lively narrative coverage of the period. Its interpretation, however, seems to me to be frequently questionable and on occasion only loosely related to the sources, and the title itself indicates that it was not conceived as an introduction. Similarly, Patricia Crone's *Slaves on horses* seems to me a brilliant analysis of the development of the early Islamic state and society but not a book for relative beginners since it presumes, rather than provides, a fairly detailed acquaintance with the events of the period. There still seems a need, therefore, for the sort of introduction which I have attempted here.

Given, then, that the present work is not attempting to provide a wholly new version of the Umayyad period, and that much of it depends on the findings of the many scholars who have contributed to our understanding of Umayyad history, it has seemed unnecessary to provide references to the original Arabic or other sources. Readers capable of studying the primary sources themselves will easily be able to track them down in the secondary works to which references are normally confined in my notes. These notes are usually a guide to further reading, with readers of English primarily in mind, and are not necessarily the sources of particular statements, but in a general way they indicate the scholars and works to which I have been most indebted. Neither the references in my notes nor the bibliography given at the end claim to be complete or extensive, but I hope that I have mentioned most works of fundamental importance.

My special thanks are due to my colleague Dr David Morgan, who kindly read the whole typescript and whose feeling for both history and style has undoubtedly saved me from a number of blunders; to my wife Joyce who has similarly read and commented on the typescript; to Sue Harrop, the Cartographer at the School of African and Oriental Studies, University of London, for help with the maps; and to Peter Sowden who first suggested that I write the book and then gently prodded until it was done. For the remaining limitations, imperfections and errors I am responsible.

Chapter 1

Introduction: The Importance of the Umayyad Period and its Place in Islamic History

In the summer or autumn of AD 661, Mu'awiya b. Abi Sufyan, governor of Syria since 639 and already acclaimed by his Syrian followers as caliph (*khalifa*), religious and political leader of the Muslim state, entered the Iraqi garrison town of Kufa. In historical tradition this event is seen as bringing to an end a bitter period of civil war among the Arabs, achieving the reunification under one ruler of all the territories conquered by them, and initiating the caliphate of the Umayyad dynasty of which Mu'awiya was the founder. The dynasty was to rule for 90 years or so until its overthrow and replacement by that of the 'Abbasids in 749–50.

The Umayyad dynasty was the first to emerge in the Middle East following the conquest of the region by the Arabs, a conquest which had begun in the 630s and was still continuing for much of the Umayyad period. Apart from this fact, however, what was the importance of the period of Umayyad rule, a period which in its details is often complex and confusing, and how has it traditionally been regarded by Muslims in relation to the history of Islam? The answer to the first part of this question is provided by discussion of the two concepts of islamisation and arabisation, referring to two related but essentially distinct historical processes.

Islamisation

The term 'islamisation' refers both to the extension of the area under Muslim rule and to the acceptance of Islam as their religion by peoples of different faiths, but in the Umayyad period the question is further complicated by the fact that Islam itself was developing from its still to us not completely understood origins into something approaching the religion with which we are familiar. One should not imagine that Islam as we know it came fully formed out of Arabia with the Arabs at the time of their conquest of the Middle East and

1

was then accepted or rejected, as the case might be, by the non-Arab peoples. Although many of the details are obscure and often controversial, it seems clear that Islam as we know it is largely a result of the interaction between the Arabs and the peoples they conquered during the first two centuries or so of the Islamic era which began in AD 622.[1] During the Umayyad period, therefore, the spread of Islam and the development of Islam were taking place at the same time, and a discussion of islamisation has to begin with some consideration of the importance of the Umayyad period for the development of Islam.

In the first place, it was under the Umayyads that there began to emerge that class of religious scholars which eventually became the leading authority within Sunni Islam and which is chiefly respon-sible for shaping the historical and religious tradition which has come down to us. In effect, it was this class which led the development of Islam as we know it, and it is important to remember that it emerged largely in opposition to the Umayyad government. The Umayyads had their own conception of Islam, itself developing with time and different circumstances, but on the whole we see the religion from the viewpoint of the religious scholars.

In the emergence of this class the most important region was Iraq, and in Iraq Kufa was the leading centre. Other regions tended to follow its lead. Building on and reacting against the ideas and practices available in Kufa and other centres, from the second half of the Umayyad period onwards groups of Muslim scholars tried to develop and put on a sound footing what they saw as a true form of Islam. In doing so they frequently accused the Umayyads of impious or unislamic behaviour.

The main concept which these scholars developed and worked with was that of the *Sunna*. This idea went through several stages but increasingly came to be identified with the custom and practice of the Prophet Muhammad, which was to serve as the ideal norm of behaviour for his followers, and was eventually accepted as the major source of Muslim law alongside the Koran. Increasingly, Muslim ideas, practices and institutions came to be justified by reference to the *Sunna*, the words and deeds of Muhammad as transmitted by his companions to later generations. The proponents of the *Sunna* as thus understood became increasingly influential, and political and religious developments after the Umayyads had been overthrown resulted in the final crystallisation of the Sunni form of Islam with the religious scholars, the guardians of the *Sunna*, as its leading authority.[2]

Not all Muslims, though, accepted the primacy or even the legitimacy of the *Sunna*, and the Umayyad period also saw the emergence of the two other main forms of Islam, Shi'ism and Kharijism. Tradition dates the fragmentation of a previously united Islam into the three main forms which we know today (Sunnis, Shi'ites and Kharijites) to the time of the first civil war (656–61), which ended with the accession of Mu'awiya to the caliphate. However, just as the development of Sunni Islam was a slow process which only began under the Umayyads, so too Shi'ism and Kharijism were not born in one instant. They too developed in opposition to the Umayyads, in a number of distinct movements which each had individual characteristics, and again Iraq was of prime importance.

Kufa was the centre of the development of Shi'ism in the Umayyad period. As early as 670, but especially after the revolt of Mukhtar in 685–7, Kufa saw a number of movements aimed at overthrowing the Umayyads and appointing a relative of the Prophet, usually a descendant of his cousin and son-in-law 'Ali, as imam, which title the Shi'ites tend to prefer to caliph. Where these Shi'ite movements differed from one another was in the particular member of the Prophet's family whom they favoured and in certain other doctrines they developed; what they had in common was devotion to the Prophet's family and insistence that membership of it was a sine qua non for the imam. Some of them developed more extreme beliefs, such as acceptance of the imam as an incarnation of God and a doctrine of the transmigration of souls. It seems that from an early date the conquered non-Arab peoples were attracted to the Shi'ite movements, and it may be that some of their doctrines were influenced by the previous beliefs of these non-Arab supporters. Shi'ism has a long and complex history which extends well beyond the Umayyad period, but it was then that its basic character was established.[3]

The basic principle of Kharijism was a demand for piety and religious excellence as the only necessary qualification for the imam, and a rejection of the view that he should belong to the family of the Prophet, as the Shi'ites demanded, or to the tribe of the Prophet (Quraysh), as the Sunnis required. Like Shi'ism, Kharijism too was manifested in a number of movements, some relatively moderate and others more extreme. The extremists tended to insist on the rejection of all other Muslims, regarding them as infidels and therefore liable to be killed unless they 'repented' and 'accepted Islam', that is, unless they recognised the Kharijite imam and accepted the Kharijite form of Islam. This fierce rejection of other Muslims, however, involving the duty of rebellion against what was regarded as an illegitimate government, became increasingly difficult to maintain except in areas remote from the authority of the government or in times when the authority of the government for some reason collapsed. In Basra, the second of the Iraqi garrison towns, on the other hand, a more moderate form of Kharijism was elaborated and spread to eastern Arabia and North Africa. It is this form of Kharijism which has survived into the modern world.[4]

Each of these three main Muslim groups came to hold that Islam should be open to all peoples and that all should enjoy the same status within it regarding rights and duties. The development of this idea too, of Islam as a universal religion, can be traced to the Umayyad period, again in circles opposed to the dynasty.

Although it can be debated whether the Koran was addressed to all men or to the Arabs only, the Umayyads and the Arab tribesmen who first conquered the Middle East regarded their religion as largely exclusive of the conquered peoples. There was no sustained attempt to force or even persuade the conquered peoples to accept Islam, and it was assumed that they would remain in their own communities paying taxes to support the conquerors. Although from the start there was some movement of the conquered into the community of the conquerors, the separation of Arabs from non-Arabs was a basic principle of the state established as a result of the conquests. This is clear both from the procedure which a non-Arab had to adopt in order to enter Islam and from the fact that there were, from time to time, official measures designed to prevent such changes of status. Islam was in fact regarded as the property of the conquering aristocracy.

In order to attach himself to the religion and society of the Arabs, a non-Arab had to become the client (*mawla*, pl. *mawali*) of an Arab tribe. In other words, in order to become a Muslim, something which it is possible to see as a social or political as much as a religious move, he had to acquire an Arab patron and become a sort of honorary member of his patron's tribe, adding the tribal name to his own new Muslim one, even though he and his descendants were in some ways treated as second-class Muslims. It is evident, therefore, that membership of Islam was equated with possession of an Arab ethnic identity.[5]

Nevertheless, association with the elite in this way did have advantages for some, and at various times in different places we hear of large numbers of non-Arabs attempting to enter Islam by becoming *mawali* but being prevented from doing so, or at least from having their changed status recognised, by local Umayyad governors. Probably the best-known example was in Iraq around 700 when large numbers of local non-Arab cultivators sought to abandon their lands and flee into the Arab garrison towns to enter Islam as *mawali*, only to be forced back by the Umayyad governor al-Hajjaj who refused to recognise their claims.

In the long run it proved impossible to maintain the isolation of conquerors and conquered from one another in this way, and attempts to do so only served to alienate further those Muslim groups which had come to see Islam as a religion open to all. The problem for the Umayyads was that they had come to power as leaders of a conquering Arab elite and to have allowed the conquered peoples to enter Islam *en masse* would have abolished or at least weakened the distinction between the elite and the masses. The crucial privileges of Islam, from this point of view, were in the area of taxation. In principle the Arabs were to be the recipients of the taxes paid by the non-Arabs. If the conquered peoples were allowed to become Muslims, and to change their position from that of payers to that of recipients of taxes, the whole system upon which the Umayyads depended would collapse. But as the pressure from the non-Arabs built up, and the universalist notion of Islam became stronger, this problem became increasingly urgent for the dynasty and played a major part in the generally negative attitude of Muslims towards the Umayyad dynasty.[6]

How far the development of Islam in the Umayyad period involved radical changes in religious practices or beliefs is not easy to say. Broadly speaking, Muslim tradition assumes that the fundamental institutions of Islam — such things as belief in Muhammad as a prophet, acceptance of the Koran in the form in which we know it as the word of God, and performance of the main rituals such as the five times daily prayer (*salat*) and the annual pilgrimage to Mecca (*hajj*) — existed at the beginning of the Umayyad period and were accepted equally by the Umayyads and their opponents. The difficulty is to decide how far our Muslim sources, which are relatively late in the form in which we have them, are reading back later conditions into an earlier period.

Sometimes, certainly, we have hints that the situation was not so static or so uniform as the tradition generally implies. For example we are told that Muslim rebels supporting Ibn al-Ash'ath against the Umayyads in the early years of the eighth century accused the caliph of 'murdering' the ritual prayer (*salat*) and called for vengeance for it, although what this meant and what exactly was involved, if anything specific, is not spelled out.[7] Even such tantalisingly obscure hints are relatively scarce, and when we do sometimes have more substantial information its significance seems often to be limited in one of two ways.

First, the information may centre on a point which seems to be relatively minor. For instance, much play is made with the charge that the Umayyads insisted on delivering the *khutba* (in the early period a speech or sermon given usually in the mosque by the caliph or his representative and often dealing with secular as well as more purely religious affairs) while sitting, contrary to what is alleged to have been the practice established by the Prophet and his immediate successors. This is supposed to be a sign of the haughtiness of the Umayyads, refusing to stand before their subjects and preferring, like kings, to remain seated. Even though the detail may have lost some of its significance because of the later decline in importance of the *khutba* and its associated institutions and ceremonies, however, it is difficult to see arguments about the correct posture for the *khutba* as of fundamental importance for the development of Islam. In the way in which the practice is presented by Muslim tradition, it does not provide grounds for arguing that the outward forms of Islam underwent great and radical changes under the Umayyads.[8]

Secondly, even when the information is apparently more weighty, the impression is usually given that the Umayyads were perverting some orthodox practice or belief which already existed and was widely accepted by Muslims. There is no suggestion that basic religious ideas were still in a state of flux and that 'orthodoxy' (an ambiguous term in Islam since there is no central authority to say what is and what is not orthodox) was only slowly developing. We are told, for instance, that some of the Umayyads tried to make Jerusalem a centre of pilgrimage, but the sources imply that this was against the background of an already generally accepted practice of annual pilgrimage to Mecca which had been established as the cultic centre of Islam from the time of the Prophet. The reader should be aware of such preconceptions in the sources and consider the possibility that there may not have been, as yet, any firmly established cultic centre in Islam.[9]

Any attempt to argue that there were during the Umayyad period more fundamental religious developments than the sources allow for, therefore, involves a certain amount of 'reading between the lines' of Muslim tradition and using whatever evidence is available outside the Muslim literary sources. A recent discussion using such methods has questioned whether the name 'Islam', as the designation for the religion of the Arabs, existed much before the end of the seventh century.[10] Muslim tradition itself, though, has proved remarkably impervious to analysis with such questions in mind, and one's attitude to the question of the extent of the religious development of Islam in the Umayyad period must depend greatly on one's attitude to the value of Muslim sources for the history of the period, and especially the earlier part.

The spread of Islam during this period, as already indicated, has to be viewed on two levels, that of its territorial expansion and that of its acceptance by the conquered non-Arab peoples from a variety of religious backgrounds.

Muslim tradition is generally more concerned with the former process. When an area is under Muslim rule and subject to Muslim law, that area is regarded as a part of the Muslim world (*dar al-Islam*), even though the majority of its population may remain non-Muslim. Strictly speaking, only Christians, Jews and Zoroastrians (these last known as *majus*) were to be allowed to refuse to accept Islam and maintain their existence as separate religious communities under Muslim rule, but in practice toleration was frequently extended more widely.

From this point of view, then, the extensive conquests made under the Umayyads were an extension of Islam. At the beginning of the Umayyad period Arab Muslim rule did not extend much further west than modern Libya or further east than the eastern regions of Iran, and even within these areas many regions must have been held only precariously or merely nominally. By the end of the dynasty all of North Africa and southern and central Spain were included in the boundaries of the Muslim world, and in the east the extension of control into central Asia and northern India prepared the way for later advances in those areas.

In the west the garrison town of Qayrawan was founded about 670 in Ifriqiya (modern Tunisia), and this served as the base for further westward expansion. 'Uqba b. Nafi' is subsequently said to have marched as far as the Atlantic before being killed by the still unsubdued Berbers, but it was not until the end of the century that regions of modern Algeria and Morocco were substantially pacified and the Berbers brought into Islam, but keeping their own language and tribal system. This development is associated with the governorship of Hassan b. Nu'man in Ifriqiya (683–707). It was Hassan's successor, Musa b. Nusayr, who initiated the invasion of Spain in 711, sending his Berber client (*mawla*) Tariq to lead the expedition. It is from this Tariq that Gibraltar takes its name (Jabal Tariq, 'the hill of Tariq').

In the east too the years around 700 saw major advances. Al-Hajjaj, governor of the eastern part of the Umayyad territories from 694 to 714, sent his generals Ibn al-Ash'ath against the ruler of Kabul, Qutayba b. Muslim into the territories lying beyond the river Oxus (Jayhun or Amu Darya in Muslim works), and Muhammad b. al-Qasim into northern India. Qutayba is said to have reached the borders of China and sent an embassy demanding submission from the 'king of China'. The extent and effectiveness of these expeditions may sometimes be open to question, but it is clear that Arab Muslim control was extended and consolidated in the east under the Umayyads.[11]

The spread of Islam among the non-Arab peoples of the conquered regions is much less explicitly described in our sources. At the outset of the Umayyad period it is clear that very few of the conquered peoples had accepted Islam, however we understand this last phrase (*islam* literally means 'submission'). But by the end of the period, in spite of the initial attempt by the Arabs to keep themselves apart religiously and socially from their subjects, and in spite of the refusal by caliphs and governors to allow the non-Arabs to enjoy the advantages of acceptance of Islam, large numbers of the subject peoples had come to identify themselves as Muslims.

The spread of Islam vertically in this way is clearly a complex process, depending on a variety of factors which were not the same in every area or among every group of the non-Arab population, and resulting in divergent rates of progress. Because of the silence or ambiguity of the sources we are often reduced to speculation about causes and the spread of the process. For example, we know very little about the islamisation of Syria and there are only one or two references in non-Muslim sources which seem to indicate substantial islamisation of the local peoples during the Umayyad period. On the other hand, the Muslim sources have many references to the difficulties caused to Umayyad governors of Iraq and Khurasan when large numbers of non-Arab non-Muslims attempted to accept Islam by becoming *mawali* in the early decades of the eighth century, but they still leave many questions unanswered or answered at best ambiguously.

So far as the evidence enables us to judge, and leaving aside the Berbers whose society and way of life made them likely allies for the Arabs in the wars of conquest, it seems to have been in lower Iraq, Khurasan and Syria that Islam made the most significant advances among the subjects peoples in the Umayyad period. In western Persia and Egypt, on the other hand, it seems that islamisation in this sense was relatively slow and that it was not until after the dynasty had been overthrown that Islam became the religion of the majority in these areas.[12]

In spite of our uncertainties, it seems clear that the Umayyad period was crucial for the process of Islamisation in all its forms.

Arabisation

By 'arabisation' I mean the spread of a culture characterised above all by its use of the Arabic language in the area which had become subject to Arab Muslim rule. Although associated with the process of islamisation, arabisation is a distinct movement as can be seen from the fact that important communities of Jews and Christians survived in the Islamic Middle East into modern times. These communities maintained their religious traditions in spite of the fact that they had renounced the everyday languages which they had used before the Arab conquest and had adopted Arabic. Conversely, Persia presents a striking example of a region which largely accepted Islam as its religion but maintained its pre-Islamic language at first in everyday and later in literary use, although, of course, the language underwent significant changes in the early Islamic period.

Again one has to take into account that Arabic itself changed as it spread and was elaborated in the process of interaction between Arabs and non-Arabs. Put crudely, as the non-Arab peoples adopted Arabic, so their own linguistic habits and backgrounds affected the language, leading to significant changes and to the formation of different dialects. The result of this evolution is usually described as Middle Arabic as opposed to Classical Arabic, which is identified with the language of the Koran and of the poetry which, it is claimed, originated in pre-Islamic Arabia. The origin and nature of Classical Arabic itself, though, is to some extent a topic of controversy. What led to the adoption or rejection of Arabic by non-Arabic speakers is obviously a very complex question involving consideration of political and social relationships as well as more purely linguistic ones.

In attempting to chart the progress of arabisation the difficulties again arise from the lack of explicit information on the topic in our literary sources and from the paucity of written material surviving from the Umayyad period. For instance, although it has been suggested that Jews of all sorts began to speak Arabic as early as the seventh century, the process of change must have been gradual and our earliest texts written in Judaeo-Arabic (that is, the form of Middle Arabic used by Jews and written in Hebrew rather than Arabic script) come from the ninth century. Our earliest Christian Arabic texts (Arabic written in the Greek script) have been dated to the eighth century, but there has been some argument about the dating. On the other hand, from later developments we know that Persian must have survived as the spoken language of the majority of Iranians during the Umayyad period, but our sources only rarely and ambiguously let us see that it was so, and almost all of our source material on the history of Persia under the Umayyads is in Arabic.

More concrete evidence is provided by the administrative papyri which have survived from Egypt. In spite of the limited range of subjects with which they are concerned, they at least enable us to see a gradual change from Greek to Arabic in the language of the administration. Furthermore, our literary sources report that around 700 it was ordered that henceforth the government administration should use Arabic rather than the languages which had been used before the Arab conquest and which had continued in use thus far. This could indicate that there was at that time a significant number of non-Arabs with sufficient command of Arabic at least for the purposes of administration, since the bureaucracy continued to rely overwhelmingly on non-Arabs. The change of language in the bureaucracy did not happen overnight, and the sources are not unanimous about when it was ordered, but in the development of arabisation it seems to have been a significant step.

Why and how Arabic, and with it the other features which seem to make Islamic culture in the Middle East significantly Arab and distinguish it from others, spread is, therefore, still debatable. Eventually, as we know, the adoption of Arabic for most purposes became general in Syria, Iraq and Egypt while the Berbers and Persians, in spite of their acceptance of Islam and therefore of Arabic as their sacred language, continued to use their own languages for everyday purposes. We can assume that arabisation, like islamisation, progressed a long way under the Umayyads, but precise evidence is hard to come by.[13]

The Umayyads in Muslim Tradition

The second question asked at the beginning of this chapter concerned the way in which the Umayyad dynasty has been regarded by Muslim tradition and how it has been seen in the context of Islamic history generally. Discussion of this question, which involves some consideration of the way in which our Muslim sources for the period came to be formed, is a necessary condition for an understanding of the narrative history which the remainder of this work undertakes.

Even allowing for the qualifications which will be made shortly, there is no doubt that in its broad outlines as well as in its details Muslim tradition is generally hostile to the Umayyads. When the two can be distinguished, Shi'ite tradition is more hostile than that of the Sunnis, but many of our sources contain material which reflects both Shi'ite and Sunni points of view so that there is some justification, for our purposes here, in talking about Muslim tradition as a whole.[14] The hostility of tradition is reflected in both what the tradition reports and the way in which it reports it.

We are told that before Islam the Umayyad family was prominent in the opposition to Muhammad among the Meccans and that most of the members of the family only accepted Islam at the last moment when it became clear that the Prophet was going to be victorious. Once inside the Muslim community, however, they exploited circumstances, and, by skilful political manipulation not entirely free from trickery, they obtained power, displacing those whose claims to the leadership were based on long service to Islam, piety, and relationship to the Prophet. In power they pursued policies which at best paid no regard to the requirements of Islam and at worst were positively anti-Islamic. Among the charges brought against them, some of the most prominent are that they made the caliphate hereditary within the Umayyad family; that they oppressed and even caused the death of numerous men of religion and of the Prophet's family, most notably of the Prophet's grandson Husayn; that they attacked the holy cities of Mecca and Medina, going so far as to bombard Mecca with catapults on two occasions— an image which may well symbolise the conception of the Umayyads in tradition; and that they prevented non-Muslims from accepting Islam and obtaining the rights due to them. They ruled by force and tyranny. Literary works came to be produced devoted to cataloguing the crimes of the Umayyads, singing the praises of their opponents, and explaining why God allowed the community to fall under the sway of these godless tyrants. The best-known of these works are those of Jahiz in the ninth and Maqrizi in the fifteenth centuries.[15]

Tradition expresses its hostility to the dynasty above all by insisting that they were merely kings and refusing to recognise them, with one exception, as caliphs. The caliphate, according to tradition, emerged in Medina on the death of Muhammad in order to provide a leader for the Muslims in succession to him. The title *khalifa* is interpreted as meaning 'successor of the Prophet', in full *khalifat rasul Allah*, and the caliph was to be motivated solely by the interests of the Muslims. The Muslim theory of the caliphate took time to evolve and was never static, but two ideas in particular came to be prominent. First, the caliph was to be chosen, from among those with the necessary qualifications, by some sort of election. How this election was to be carried out was never agreed on but the feeling was that the caliph should not simply seize the office by force or be appointed by one man with no consultation of the Muslims. Secondly, the caliph's authority was to be limited, in particular in the sphere of religion, where the real authorities, the guardians of the *Sunna* and the heirs of the Prophet, were the religious scholars (the *'ulama'*). In effect, the caliph was simply to maintain the conditions in which the religious scholars could get on with their task. (All this, of course, refers primarily to the Sunni view of the caliphate. The Shi'ites and Kharijites had different ideas.)[16]

A sharp distinction is then made between the idea of a caliph and that of a king, between caliphate (*khilafa*) and kingship (*mulk*). Unlike the caliph, the king (*malik*, pl. *muluk*) is an arbitrary, worldly ruler whose power depends ultimately on force. The symbolic type of king for Muslim tradition is the Byzantine emperor (*Qaysar*, i.e., 'Caesar') and the Sasanid shah (*Kisra*, i.e., 'Chosroes', 'Khusraw'). When tradition denigrates Umayyad rule as kingship, therefore, it is putting the Umayyads in the same category as all the other kings of this world and contrasting them with its own ideal of Islamic government.

It is not the personal qualities or defects of a ruler which determine primarily whether he is to be accorded the status of caliph or discarded as a king, although the personal piety or wickedness of an individual could affect the question. There were some personally upright Umayyads just as there were corrupt and debauched members of the 'Abbasid dynasty which took over the caliphate when the Umayyads were overthrown. The latter, however, are all accepted as caliphs by Sunni tradition while the former, with the one exception, are merely kings. Nor does it depend on the self-designation of the dynasty. The Umayyads do not appear to have used the title *malik* (king) and they did not, at least in the earlier Umayyad period, affect in a very marked way the paraphernalia of kingship such as a crown, throne or sceptre. In contrast to them, the early 'Abbasid rule was associated much more with the symbols of a traditional oriental despotism.[17]

In fact it was the Umayyads' use of the title *khalifa* which probably played an important part in the tradition's classification of them as kings. Whereas Muslim tradition regards the title as an abbreviation of *khalifat rasul Allah*, signifying successor of the Prophet, the Umayyads, as evidenced by coins and inscriptions, used the title *khalifat Allah*. While it is not completely impossible to reconcile the use of this title with the traditional understanding of *khalifa*, it does seem likely that the Umayyads' conception of the title and the office was different. *Khalifat Allah* (Caliph of God) almost certainly means that they regarded themselves as deputies of God rather than as mere successors to the Prophet, since it is unlikely that *khalifa* here means successor (one cannot be a successor of God) and elsewhere *khalifa* is frequently met with in the sense of deputy. In other words, the title implies that the Umayyads regarded themselves as God's representatives at the head of the community and saw no need to share their religious power with, or delegate it to, the emergent class of religious scholars.[18]

Above all the charge of kingship is connected with the decision of Mu'awiya to appoint his own son Yazid as his successor to the caliphate during his own lifetime. This event, more than anything else, seems to be behind the accusation that Mu'awiya perverted the caliphate into a kingship. The episode will be considered more fully later, but, in the light of the Sunni conception of the nature of the caliphate, what was wrong with Mu'awiya's appointment of Yazid was that one man took it upon himself to choose a caliph with no consultation with the representatives of Islam (whoever they might be) and without even a token nod to the idea that the office should be elective. It is probable that such ideas were not generally held, even if they yet existed, in the time of Mu'awiya. But according to tradition he acted as a king in this matter, introducing the hereditary principle into the caliphate, and the dynasty which he thus founded, and which maintained the general principle that the ruler nominated his successor, was thus a line of kings. Yazid's personal failings, which are certainly underlined by tradition, merely seem to reinforce the message and are not really the source of opposition to his appointment.[19]

It should be clear, then, that tradition is generally hostile to the Umayyad dynasty. It is, nevertheless, true that the same Muslim tradition transmits some material which is more ambiguous, sometimes even overtly favourable to the Umayyads. For example, the administrative and political ability of caliphs like Mu'awiya and 'Abd al-Malik is admitted, and some of the 'Abbasids are said to have expressed admiration for this aspect of their predecessors' work. Even on more strictly religious questions, the tradition sometimes seems less clear-cut than one would expect. The name 'the year of the (reestablishment of the) community', which is applied both to the year in which Mu'awiya received acknowledgment in Kufa after his defeat of 'Ali and to that in which 'Abd al-Malik similarly ended the second civil war, recognises the virtues of these two caliphs in rescuing the community from a period of internal dissension. Indeed, one often finds in tradition a fearfulness for the fate of the community under such enemies of the Umayyads as 'Ali and Ibn al-Zubayr, whatever their personal merits might have been. In legal traditions some Umayyads, notably Marwan, himself caliph for a short time and ancestor of one of the two branches of the Umayyad family to acquire the caliphate, are frequently referred to as makers of legal rulings, and they often come out quite favourably even in comparison with some of the most important of the Prophet's companions. On occasion a maxim which one tradition ascribes to, say, Marwan will appear elsewhere as a maxim of the Prophet himself. Even the bombardment of Mecca and the consequent damage to the Ka'ba, which is a key point in the traditional complaints against the dynasty, can be toned down. Among the various reports of these events, some say that the fire which damaged the Ka'ba while Mecca was being bombarded came about accidentally, and some even say that it was caused by the carelessness of one of the defenders of Mecca, even Ibn al-Zubayr himself being named. Here we are not concerned with the historical accuracy of these reports, merely with the fact that they are transmitted even though the tenor of Muslim tradition is broadly anti-Umayyad.[20]

Even the treatment of the one Umayyad caliph who is recognised as such in tradition and exempted from the accusation of kingship levelled at the others, 'Umar b. 'Abd al-'Aziz ('Umar II, 717–20), may be ambiguous. In one way to nominate him as the only caliph in a line of kings serves, of course, to underline the contrast between the pious 'Umar and the rest of the dynasty, but equally it could be argued that the existence of 'Umar to some extent rescues the dynasty from complete condemnation. While the traditions about him emphasise the links on his mother's side with 'Umar I, the second successor of Muhammad and one of the four Rightly Guided Caliphs, they also do not hide the fact that on his father's side he was a leading member of the Umayyad family. His father was brother of the caliph 'Abd al-Malik and governor of Egypt for most of the latter's caliphate. Evidently, therefore, the Umayyads could produce a genuine caliph and one could conclude that there was nothing inherently bad in the family.[21]

In order to understand both the generally negative attitude towards the Umayyads in Muslim tradition and the fact that the tradition transmits material which is apparently more favourable to the dynasty, it is necessary to understand the way in which the tradition came to be formed — the way in which our Muslim literary sources originated, were transmitted, collected and finally committed to writing in the form in which we know them.

It seems likely that it was not until the later part of the Umayyad period that traditions, religious or historical (and the distinction is not always clear), came to be committed to writing with any frequency. Before that time they were generally transmitted orally in short, separate reports which were self-contained and relatively easy to memorise. As it became more common to put them in a written form, however, these short reports could be united into more complex units, compiled around a theme or organised in a narrative framework. In the later Umayyad and early 'Abbasid period, then, scholars such as Abu Mikhnaf (d. 774), Ibn Ishaq (d. 761), or 'Awana (d. 764) began to compile 'books' by collecting the traditions available and organising them around a theme such as the battle of the Camel, the second civil war, or even the history of the caliphate. They may have simply dictated the relevant material to their disciples, which would account for the different versions of works attributed to a particular scholar which have come down to us from different disciples, or they may have put it in writing themselves.

The material thus collected was then transmitted to later generations which treated it in a variety of ways. It might be again broken up and put together with material from different sources in order to make it relate to a different theme; long narratives might be abridged by omitting material considered irrelevant; short narratives might be filled out by interpolation or by linking material together without making it clear where the link occurs or even that it has been made; material might fall out of circulation or it might be reshaped consciously or subconsciously by substitution of words or phrases, by the addition of glosses, or even by formulating entirely new material. It is obvious, therefore, that there was plenty of scope for the material to change in the course of its transmission, and it would be natural that it should change in accordance with changing political, social and religious circumstances. Generally speaking, the material would have been constantly revised to make it relevant and acceptable, and the original significance and context of the material would come to be forgotten.

This process continued for some generations until, in the ninth and tenth centuries, written versions of the material were produced which have survived as our earliest Muslim literary sources, our earliest examples of Muslim historical writing, biography, Koranic exegesis, and so on. In fact, of course, the process continued even beyond the ninth and tenth centuries: even in the fifteenth and sixteenth centuries Muslim scholars were selecting from and reshaping the works of their predecessors, but, when we have the material in both its early and its later form, we can clearly see what has happened to it in the course of transmission. Our problem with our earliest sources for the Umayyad period is that the material prior to the ninth and tenth centuries has been lost and we have to depend on relatively late versions of it transmitted to us by scholars such as Baladhuri (d. 892) and Tabari (d. 923).[22]

An important point is that a decisive role in the collection, transmission and reduction to writing of the material was played by scholars representative of the opposition to the Umayyads. That is, scholars associated with the Muslim circles hostile to the dynasty, predominantly in Iraq, took a leading role in collecting, arranging and editing the material. If we add to this the fact that the written material which has come down to us was produced in the period after the Umayyads had been overthrown, under the caliphate of the 'Abbasids who had supplanted them, it is not hard to understand why it has the fundamental hostility to the Umayyads which has been indicated. It is not a question of the 'Abbasids employing scholars to produce deliberate justifications for 'Abbasid rule, rather that the scholars involved inherited material from, and were themselves part of the tradition of, Muslim opposition to the Umayyads.

Although we often refer to scholars like Baladhuri and Tabari as historians inasmuch as they were concerned with producing a picture of the past and its relationship to their own times, objectivity, which has been regarded as at least a desideratum of the historian since the nineteenth century, is not to be expected from them. Fundamentally they were religious scholars and it is useful to remember that Tabari, whose *Ta'rikh* (a mixture of history and chronicle) is one of our fullest sources of information on early Islam and the Umayyad period, wrote a Koranic commentary which is even more voluminous and which, regarding the life of Muhammad, often provides more 'historical' information than is available in the *Ta'rikh*.

If the outlook of these scholars was likely to make them generally hostile to the Umayyads, however, certain things mitigated this hostility and help to explain the more ambiguous material which has been noted. Most importantly, the material collected and transmitted by any individual scholar may be traced ultimately to a wide variety of sources, including even pro-Umayyad sources, and there was no central directory imposing a censorship on the scholars. It used to be thought, following Wellhausen, that the scholars could all be classified as the representatives of one or another 'school', that the material associated with the name of a particular scholar would be biased to support the geographical and religious viewpoint of the 'school' to which he belonged. So Abu Mikhnaf was regarded as a representative of the Iraqis, Ibn Ishaq of the Medinese, and so on. But it is now recognised that one will find many different shades of opinion represented in the material transmitted under the name of any individual. Even the earliest of them already had an amount of material from which to select, and we cannot point to a particular time or individual as being decisive in the formation of the tradition. Any analysis of the tradition needs to take into account both its final editing and arranging and its earlier transmission.[23]

Secondly, the scholars were strongly aware of the element of continuity in the history of Islam, and to have been too hostile to the Umayyads, portraying them as non-Muslims for example, would have been incompatible with this sense of continuity. It may be that the traditions about 'Umar II, linking the Umayyads with the period of Rightly Guided Caliphs, are particularly influenced by this sense of continuity. Those scholars representing the Sunni tendency had a particular problem. If the legitimacy of the Umayyads was questioned too sharply, ammunition might be provided for the Shi'ites, most of whom came to see 'Ali as having been cheated not only by Mu'awiya but also by the first two caliphs, Abu Bakr and 'Umar, who are of central importance for the Sunni concept of the transmission of the Prophet's Sunna to the later community. Furthermore, Mu'awiya himself was a companion of Muhammad, his secretary according to tradition, and one of the characteristics of Sunni Islam is its championing of the companions as sources of authoritative teaching, as against the Shi'ites who viewed them in general with suspicion and as enemies of 'Ali and the imams.

Muslim tradition is virtually our only detailed source for the history of the Umayyad state. It should be obvious, therefore, that the nature of the tradition has to be borne in mind constantly when attempting to discuss the history of the period.

For modern treatment of the Umayyads, see Appendix 2.

Notes

1. C. H. Becker was one of the first to insist on the distinction between islamisation and arabisation, and he stressed too the crucial importance for the development of Islam as we know it of the interaction between Arabs and conquered peoples outside Arabia in the period after the Arab conquests. See his *Islamstudien*, i, 66–145, and in English his 'The expansion of the Saracens' in the *Cambridge Mediaeval History*, 1st edition 1911–36, ii, chapters 11 and 12.

2. This understanding of the emergence of the schools of religious scholars and their elaboration of the notion of *Sunna* depends on the results of J. Schacht's persuasive, but still controversial, studies of early Muslim jurisprudence. See his *Introduction to Islamic law*, especially chapters 5 and 6, and the article 'Fikh' in *EI2*; for a more conservative analysis of the concept of *Sunna*, taking issue with Schacht, M. M. Bravmann, *The spiritual background*, 179 ff.; R. B. Serjeant in *Arabic literature to*

the end of the Umayyad period, ed. A. F. L. Beeston *et al.*, Cambridge 1983, 142–7.

3. J. Wellhausen, *The religio-political factions in early Islam*; M. Hodgson, 'How did the early Shi'a become sectarian?', *JAOS*, 75 (1955); S. Moscati, 'Per una storia dell' antica Ši'a', *RSO*, 30 (1955); W. M. Watt, 'Shi'ism under the Umayyads', *JRAS*, (1960); W. F. Tucker, 'Bayan b. Sam'an and the Bayaniyya: Shi'ite extremists of Umayyad Iraq', *MW*, 65 (1975); *idem*, 'Rebels and gnostics: al-Mugira ibn Sa'id and the Mugiriyya', *Arabica*, 22 (1975); *idem*, 'Abu Mansur al-'Ijli and the Mansuriyya: a study in medieval terrorism', *Isl.*, 54 (1977); *idem*, "Abd Allah b. Mu'awiya and the Janahiyya: rebels and ideologues of the late Umayyad period', *SI*, 51 (1980); S. M. Jafri, *The origins and early development of Shi'a Islam*.

4. J. Wellhausen, *Factions*; W. Thomson, 'Kharijitism and the Kharijites', in *The MacDonald presentation volume*, Princeton and London 1933; W. M. Watt, 'Kharijite thought in the Umayyad period', *Isl.*, 36 (1961); articles 'Azarika', 'Ibadiyya' and 'Kharijites' in *EI2*.

5. I. Goldziher, *Muslim Studies*, i, 101 ff.; P. Crone, *Slaves on horses*, 49–57.

6. See pp. 70–1,76–81, 85–6, 105–7.

7. See p. 70.

8. I Goldziher, *Muslim Studies*, ii, 49 ff.; H. Lammens, *Mo'awia Ier*, 202 ff.; on the development of the *khutba* and associated features, article 'Khutba' in *EI2*.

9. Cf. I. Goldziher, *Muslim Studies*, ii, 48 ff. and S. D. Goitein, 'The sanctity of Jerusalem and Palestine' in his *Studies in Islamic history and institutions*.

10. P. Crone and M. A. Cook, *Hagarism*, 8, 19–20.

11. C. H. Becker, 'The expansion of the saracens'; H. A. R. Gibb, *The Arab conquests in central Asia*; F. McGraw Donner, *The early Islamic conquests*.

12. D. C. Dennett, *Conversion and the poll-tax in early Islam*; M. Lapidus, 'The conversion of Egypt to Islam', *IOS*, (1972); M. Brett, 'The islamisation of North Africa', *Islam and modernisation in North Africa*, ed. M. Brett; N. Levtzion (ed.), *Conversion to Islam*; R. Bulliet, *Conversion to Islam in the medieval period*.

13. A Poliak, 'L'arabisation de l'orient semitique', *REI*, 12 (1938); M. Sprengling, 'Persian into Arabic', *AJSL* (1939, 1940); J. Blau, *The emergence and linguistic background of Judaeo-Arabic*; article "Arabiyya" in *EI2*; G. Lazard, 'The rise of the New Persian language', in R. N. Frye (ed.), *The Cambridge History of Iran*, iv, London 1975.

14. For Shi'ite views of the Umayyads, E. Kohlberg, 'Some Imami Shi'i interpretations of Umayyad history', in G. H. A. Juynboll (ed.), *Studies on the first century of Islamic society*, 145 ff.

15. Jahiz, *Risala fi Bani Umayya* (=*Risala fi'l-nabita*), French trans. Ch. Pellat, *AIEOr. Alger* (1952); Maqrizi, *Al-Niza' wa'l-takhasum fima bayna Bani Umayya wa-Bani Hashim*, English trans. C. E. Bosworth, *Al-Maqrizi's 'Book of contention and strife'*.

16. Article 'Khalifa' in *EI2*; for discussion of one of the most important statements of the qualifications, powers and duties of the caliph, see H. A. R. Gibb, 'Al-Mawardi's theory of the *khilafa*' in his *Studies on the civilization of Islam*.

17. I. Goldziher, *Muslim Studies*, ii, 38 ff.; G. E. von Grunebaum, *Medieval Islam*, 156 ff.; A. Abel, 'Le Khalife, presence sacrée', *SI*, 7 (1957); O. Grabar, 'Notes sur les ceremonies umayyades', in *Studies in memory of Gaston Wiet*, ed. Myriam Rosen-Ayalon, Jerusalem 1977.

18. Cf. I. Goldziher, 'Du sens propre des expressions Ombre de Dieu, etc.' *RHR*, 35 (1897); W. M. Watt, 'God's caliph. Quranic interpretations and Umayyad claims' in *Iran and Islam*, ed. C. E. Bosworth, Edinburgh 1971.

19. Note that it is Mu'awiya rather than Yazid who bears the brunt of the charge of corrupting the *khalifa* to *mulk*.

20. G. R. Hawting, 'The Umayyads and the Hijaz', *Proceedings of the fifth seminar for Arabian Studies*, London 1972.

21. C. H. Becker, 'Studien zur Omajjadengeschichte. a) 'Omar II', *ZA*, 15 (1900).

22. Article 'Ta'rikh' in *EI1 Supplement*; P. Crone, *Slaves on horses*, 'Historiographical introduction'; A. A. Duri, *The rise of historical writing among the Arabs.*

23. A Noth, *Quellenkritische Studien zu Themen, Formen, und Tendenzen frühislamischen Geschichtsüberlieferung.*

Chapter 2

The Umayyad Family and its Rise to the Caliphate

The Background of the Umayyads

According to Muslim tradition, the Umayyad family is part of that subdivision of the Arab people which is descended ultimately from the biblical Ishmael (Isma'il in Arabic) the son of Abraham (Ibrahim). The Muslim genealogical tradition divides the Arab people into two main groups which for convenience we may call 'northerners' and 'southerners', referring to the areas of Arabia which are regarded as their homelands. The 'southerners' are held to be descended from the biblical Joktan (Qahtan), a descendant of Noah, while Ishmael is the father of the 'northerners'. Among the many tribal groups of whom Ishmael is seen as the ancestor was that of Quraysh, and the Umayyad family was a sub-group of Quraysh.[1]

In the pre-Islamic period Quraysh had settled in Mecca and taken control of the town together with its ancient sanctuary, the Ka'ba, which, tradition tells us, Abraham had built at God's command. In the course of time the Arabs had corrupted Abraham's sanctuary and adopted polytheistic beliefs and practices, although they still regarded the Ka'ba as the most important sanctuary of Arabia and pilgrims came to it from nearly all the Arab tribes. It was one of the main tasks of the Prophet Muhammad at the beginning of the seventh century to purify the Ka'ba and restore its cult to the worship of the one true God. Muhammad himself was, like the Umayyads, a member of the tribe of Quraysh, and so too were the 'Abbasids, the family which eventually displaced the Umayyads as caliphs. Indeed it seems to have become accepted quite early by most Muslims that only members of Quraysh could aspire to the office of caliph or imam.[2]

The specific descent of the Umayyads within the wider grouping of Quraysh begins with a certain 'Abd Shams, son of 'Abd Manaf of the tribe of Quraysh. The Umayyad family is sometimes designated by the slightly more general expression *Banu* (that is, descendants

21

of) 'Abd Shams. From 'Abd Manaf to the Prophet Muhammad Muslim tradition counts five generations. If the names refer to real historical persons, therefore, 'Abd Manaf must have lived about the second half of the fifth century. Among other offspring, 'Abd Manaf is said to be the father of twin sons, one of whom was 'Abd Shams and the other Hashim. In tradition these are the most important of 'Abd Manaf's descendants for, while 'Abd Shams was the ancestor of the Umayyads, Hashim begat a line which included the Prophet Muhammad, his son-in-law and cousin 'Ali, whom most Shi'ite Muslims regard as the only rightful leader (imam) of the community after the death of the Prophet, and the 'Abbasids.[3]

It should not be surprising, then, that the traditions about the relations between 'Abd Shams and Hashim and between their descendants often seem to prefigure the hostility which existed in Islamic times between the Umayyads and the descendants of Hashim. Since Muslim tradition generally supports the Banu Hashim against the Umayyads, the stories about their pre-Islamic history usually glorify the former at the expense of the latter. So we are told that 'Abd Shams and Hashim were Siamese twins who had to be separated by cutting. The blood that thus flowed between them at their birth was a symbol of future events. Just as, in the book of Genesis, Esau lost his birthright to his younger twin Jacob, so 'Abd Shams, who emerged from his mother before Hashim, failed to obtain the wealth, prestige and influence which accrued to Hashim. The son of 'Abd Shams, Umayya, eponym of the Umayyad family, was notably unable to match the generosity of his uncle Hashim, and as a result Hashim obtained the prestigious offices of supplying food and drink to the pilgrims who came to Mecca. These offices were two of a number associated with the Ka'ba which had been handed down in the family to which 'Abd Manaf belonged. In the Islamic period the right of providing drink for the pilgrims was still associated with the Banu Hashim.[4]

In spite of this, by the time of Muhammad it was the descendants of 'Abd Shams who were in positions of wealth and power while the Banu Hashim was less to the fore. The Umayyads in fact appear as one of the leading families of Mecca at this period and by 624 they had become the leading Meccan family and, as such, leader of the Meccan opposition to Muhammad. 624 was the date of the first great victory of Muhammad and the Muslims over the still pagan Meccans at the battle of Badr. The leader of the Umayyad family at the time, Abu Sufyan, is said to have opposed the decision taken by other leading Meccans to engage the Muslims in battle and consequently after the defeat he alone was able to preserve some prestige. Abu Sufyan, the head of the Umayyads, henceforth appears as the director of pagan Meccan opposition to Muhammad and Islam, an image which would naturally appeal to later Muslim opponents of the Umayyad caliphs.

The opposition to Muhammad was, as we know, doomed to failure. By 629 he was able with his followers to occupy Mecca almost without fighting and receive the submission of most of these Meccans who still maintained their hostility to him and his religion. Already before this event, we are told, Abu Sufyan and other prominent Meccans, among them his son Mu'awiya, had begun, seeing which way the wind was blowing, to go over to Muhammad, sometimes secretly. Naturally, these 'conversions' are the subject of many, frequently variant, accounts, differing parties wanting to make them earlier or later, providing attendant circumstances which confirm or call into question their sincerity, and so forth. It is generally accepted, however, that the fall of Mecca ended Meccan opposition to Islam and that Abu Sufyan and his family, notably his sons Yazid and Mu'awiya, accepted Islam by this date at the latest.

A derogatory expression which is sometimes used in Muslim tradition to refer to the Umayyads is *al-tulaqa'*, 'the freedmen'. This is explained by the fact that the conquest of Mecca had made them slaves of Muhammad but he had chosen to set them free. However, tradition also reports that the Prophet was eager to secure and reinforce the allegiance of his former enemies like Abu Sufyan and, to this end, he made them special gifts after his conquest of Mecca, a tactic known as the 'winning of the hearts' (*ta'līf al-qulūb*).[5]

One might have expected that the triumph of Islam in Mecca would lead to the disappearance of the former pagan leaders from positions of power and influence, but, while positions of central power certainly passed to figures known for their early and genuine acceptance of Islam, it seems that the former Meccan pagan nobility had qualities which were useful to the new order. We are told that Abu Sufyan himself was given positions of authority in the Yemen and in Ta'if even while the Prophet was still alive, and his sons Yazid and Mu'awiya were put in command of some of the raiding forces sent to Syria after the Prophet's death. When Syria eventually fell to the Arabs following the battle of Yarmuk in 636 and its Byzantine rulers were driven out, Yazid, the son of Abu Sufyan, became its second governor and, when he died soon afterwards, he was succeeded by his brother Muʻawiya in 639. It was from this position as governor of Syria that Muʻawiya, some fifteen years later, was to launch the campaign which brought him to the caliphate.

This summary of the fortunes of the Umayyads in the pre-Islamic period and through into the early years of the Islamic era raises questions about authenticity which are probably insoluble. The image of the Umayyads as leading opponents of the Prophet and Islam, their late and opportunisitic acceptance of the new religion, and the antiquity of the rivalry between them and the Banu Hashim, all seem possible creations, or at least elaborations, of political and religious feelings against the Umayyads which developed during the course of their caliphate. Equally, the items of tradition which are more favourable towards the Umayyads, such as the story that Abu Sufyan lost an eye in the service of Islam and the Prophet promised him an eye in Paradise in compensation, or that it was Abu Sufyan's battle cry which aroused the spirit of the Muslims at a crucial time in the conquest of Syria, could be remnants of pro-Umayyad propaganda during their caliphate or later. It seems best, therefore, to accept the above as a summary of what Muslim tradition tells us and to leave open the question of its basis in fact.[6]

Muʻawiya's Acquisition of the Caliphate

Muʻawiya became caliph and founder of the Umayyad dynasty as a result of the events of a period of about five years, between 656 and 661, during which the Arabs were divided into several camps each hostile to the others. These internal hostilities led on a number of occasions to the outbreak of fighting among the recent conquerors of the heartlands of the Middle East. Muslim tradition knows this period as the *Fitna* ('time of trial'), or Great *Fitna* to distinguish it from other, later periods of internecine conflict between Muslims. Modern writers usually refer to it as the first civil war of Islam. The *Fitna* came to be seen as a period of crucial importance and as the end of something like a Golden Age in the history of Islam: not only did it give rise to the Umayyad caliphate, it is traditionally regarded as the time when the three major Muslim sects — Sunnis, Shiʻites and Kharijites — emerged from what had previously been a united community.[7]

In Muslim historical tradition the disputes of the *Fitna* appear largely as rivalries between different personalities, centring on the question of who was the legitimate caliph and what were to be his powers. Modern scholars have sought to get behind this surface explanation and to uncover the social, political and religious tensions which came to breaking point at this time. In a general way, it seems clear that the *Fitna* was the result of tensions which developed among the Arabs as they were faced with the tremendous changes to their way of life associated with their rapid conquest of large areas of the Middle East, but individual scholars have emphasised different tensions. Some, like Wellhausen, stressed the rivalries which developed among the leading circle of Muslims in Medina, between the Meccans and Medinese among the Muslim elite, and between the more pious early Muslims and the later, opportunist converts like most of the Umayyads.

Another approach, followed notably by H. A. R. Gibb, has been to stress the developing opposition between the tribesmen who made up the conquering armies, with their customary strong independence and primitive democracy, and the demands of the emerging central governmental institution headed by the caliph. The conflict between the two is seen to focus on the problem of what should be done with the land which was conquered. Should it, as the conquering tribesmen wanted, be shared out among those who had conquered it, or should it be treated as communal property for the benefit of all the Muslims, left to be cultivated by those who had done so before its conquest, and taxed by the state which would then share out or keep the proceeds as the caliph and his advisors saw fit? The latter solution, we are told, was adopted by the caliph 'Umar (634–44). Gibb argued that in 'Umar's time the conquests were in full spate and the conquering tribesmen failed to understand the significance of his decision since they were still taking vast amounts of movable booty (slaves, wealth, livestock, and so on) and did not need the land itself. After 'Umar's death, however, the pace of conquest began to slow down, the acquisition of movable booty decreased, and the tribesmen began to resent the fact that the land which they had conquered had been taken away from them. Discontent among the tribesmen against the caliph, then, was the most important element in the outbreak of the *Fitna*, and the tension between the tribesmen and the government was its main theme.

More recently Hinds and Shaban have argued that we should concentrate on divisions among the tribesmen themselves. They have focused on the situation in the garrison towns and have discerned rivalries between those who took part in the original conquests and settlements and the newcomers who migrated from Arabia in the wake of the first conquests. These rivalries were exacerbated as the government tried to increase its control over the tribesmen by supporting the authority of leading tribal notables, who had usually arrived after the first conquests, against the leaders of lesser stature who had established their positions in the garrison towns earlier. Hinds in particular has produced a body of evidence which is impressive for its cohesiveness, but here we can leave aside detailed consideration of these arguments and concentrate on the importance of the *Fitna* for the Umayyads.[8]

We have seen that Muslim tradition portrays the Umayyads generally as late and rather reluctant in their acceptance of Islam. This generalisation, though, is subject to at least one notable exception. 'Uthman b. 'Affan was both a descendant of Umayya and an early Muslim, and after the death of the Prophet he was one of the inner circle which directed the affairs of the emergent Muslim state. In 644 he was chosen as the third caliph following the death of 'Umar. Although an Umayyad, 'Uthman is not counted as one of the Umayyad dynasty since he was chosen by the inner circle of early Muslims, owed his election to his status as an early Muslim, and made no attempt to appoint an Umayyad as his successor.

It was under 'Uthman that the Golden Age of early Islam began to become tarnished and the crisis which was to issue in civil war and the irrevocable division of the community developed. Opposition to him arose in several quarters, particularly in the garrison towns, and finally in the summer of 656 a band of tribesmen from the Egyptian garrison town of Fustat came to Medina where, after the failure of negotiations, they attacked and killed 'Uthman in his house.

There are a number of possible explanations for the rise of opposition to 'Uthman, and Muslim tradition preserves whole lists of accusations made against him by his opponents. Prominent among these accusations is the charge that he practised nepotism by appointing his Umayyad relatives to important offices in the state. Indeed we are told that, in addition to confirming Mu'awiya as governor of Syria, 'Uthman appointed Umayyads to governorates in Egypt, Kufa and Basra, and that he gave the important office of keeper of the caliphal seal to another relative, the father of the future Umayyad caliph Marwan. This has been interpreted as being no more than a way in which 'Uthman sought to increase his personal control in the provinces at a time when important administrative problems were arising, but more traditionally it has been seen as a result of a weakness in his personality and the ability of his clever and unscrupulous family to exploit this weakness. However we interpret it, tradition shows us the Umayyads to some extent rebuilding under 'Uthman the influence and power which they had had before Islam.[9]

'Uthman's murder was followed by the choice of 'Ali, cousin and son-in-law of the Prophet, as the next caliph. His appointment, however, was by no means universally welcomed: personal and political rivalries existed, and his opponents were able to use the circumstances in which he had come to power — following a killing which his opponents declared unjustified, and with the support of those who had carried out the killing — to impugn his legitimacy, even though he was not charged with having personally taken part in the murder of 'Uthman. 'Uthman's Umayyad relations were prominent in the opposition to 'Ali, but the first active resistance came, not from them, but from other Qurashis resentful of 'Ali's rise to power. The leaders of this first opposition to 'Ali were 'A'isha, the widow of Muhammad, and Talha and Al-Zubayr, former companions of Muhammad and members of the inner circle at the centre of the state.

At the end of 656 they marched from Mecca, where they had first proclaimed their hostility to 'Ali, to Basra in Iraq, where they raised an army to fight against him. Learning of this, 'Ali too left the Hijaz (never again the centre of the caliphate) and came to the other Iraqi garrison town, Kufa, where he raised an army to fight the dissidents. The two forces met, in December 656, outside Basra in a battle known in tradition as the battle of the Camel, so called because the fighting wheeled around the camel upon which 'A'isha sat in her litter. The result was a complete victory for 'Ali; Talha and al-Zubayr were killed, and 'A'isha taken off back to Medina to be held in limited confinement there.[10]

The chronology and exact course of events are somewhat vague, but generally tradition puts Mu'awiya's decision to come out openly against 'Ali only after the battle of the Camel. At first, we are told, he limited himself to impugning 'Ali's legitimacy, demanding that those who had killed 'Uthman be handed over for punishment in accordance with the law of blood vengeance, and arousing among his Syrian Arab supporters fury at 'Uthman's murder. Although not the closest relative of the murdered caliph, Mu'awiya was the Umayyad with the strongest power base, having governed Syria for about fifteen years and, furthermore, being free from suspicion of having benefited from 'Uthman's alleged nepotism since he owed his appointment in Syria to 'Uthman's predecessor, the venerable 'Umar. At this time Mu'awiya was not claiming the caliphate for himself, merely demanding vengeance for 'Uthman and questioning 'Ali's right to rule. In the spring of 657 'Ali marched north from Kufa on campaign against Mu'awiya and the latter, who had been attempting to wrest Egypt from 'Ali's governor, headed for Mesopotamia to meet him.

The two met at Siffin, a site which has not been securely identified but which seems to have been in the vicinity of Raqqa but on the right bank of the Euphrates. It was late spring or early summer, and we are told that the armies faced each other for some time before fighting commenced. Then, according to the Muslim reports (contradicted by the Byzantine chronicler Theophanes), 'Ali's men were on the point of victory when there occurred an episode which has become famous. What happened is to some extent obscure but it is generally accepted that Mu'awiya's men raised copies or parts of the Koran on the ends of their spears and 'Ali's men, or the more pious among them, seeing this, forced 'Ali to stop fighting and enter into negotiation with Mu'awiya.

Whether the raising of the Korans was intended as a general reminder that both parties were Muslims and should not be fighting one another, or whether it was intended as a more specific signal that the dispute should be resolved by reference to the Word of God, is not clear, but there is a tendency to see it as no more than a ruse by the Syrians to get out of a difficult situation. The idea of it is credited, not to Mu'awiya himself, but to his right-hand man, 'Amr b. al-'As. 'Amr, who had previously led the Arab conquest of Egypt and had served as governor there before being removed by 'Uthman, was not himself an Umayyad but another of those Meccans whose acceptance of Islam was regarded as opportunistic. During the *Fitna* he appears rather as Mu'awiya's evil genius, though this is perhaps a device to save the reputation of Mu'awiya to some extent, and the implication is that he supported Mu'awiya in order to win back the governorship of Egypt. The essence of the trick of the raising of the Korans is that 'Amr is supposed to have realised that 'Ali's army included a large number of religious enthusiasts (the so called *qurra'*) and that sight of the Scripture would cause them to waver in their determination to fight.

Whatever the truth of the matter, the episode is said to have led to the breaking off of the fighting. Discussions were held and the two sides agreed to put their dispute to arbitration. Each side was to name a representative and, at an agreed time and place, the two representatives were to meet and arbitrate the dispute. Like the raising of the Korans, the arbitration too has become famous. Mu'awiya appointed 'Amr b. al-'As as his representative while 'Ali chose a former governor of Kufa and early Muslim with a reputation for piety, Abu Musa al-Ash'ari.

Why 'Ali chose Abu Musa is something of a problem. He had been governor of Kufa when 'Ali arrived there in pursuit of 'A'isha, Talha and al-Zubayr before the battle of the Camel, and he had made it clear that he did not want to become involved in the *Fitna*, advising the Kufans to remain aloof. After 'Ali gained possession of Kufa, Abu Musa was forced to leave the town. Now, however, we find him chosen as 'Ali's representative in the vital arbitration process. The only explanation which appears to make sense is that he was forced upon 'Ali by those pious followers who had been instrumental in getting him to accept the arbitration principle in the first place.

The traditions about the meeting of the arbitrators are confused and often contradictory. For one thing, it is not at all clear what they were to discuss. Was it merely the question of the legitimacy of 'Uthman's murder, or the choice of a caliph? For another, how was the arbitration to proceed? We are told that the Book of God and the *Sunna* were to be examined, but this raises questions about the significance of these terms at such an early date and how they were to provide answers for the problems facing the Muslims. Different dates and places for the meeting of the arbitrators are given, and this has led some to suggest that they met more than once and in different places. There is general agreement that the arbitration was inconclusive and that it broke up in disarray, but the reports about it do not really make sense. Abu Musa is said to have been tricked by 'Amr b. al-'As into publicly abandoning his support for 'Ali on the understanding that 'Amr would abandon his support for Mu'awiya, but, after Abu Musa had fulfilled his side of the bargain, 'Amr refused to honour his side. It has been pointed out that if such a blatant piece of trickery did occur, it would have been easy for 'Ali and his supporters to refuse to accept any outcome of the arbitration.

In any case, the arbitration does not appear to have had much importance for the further development of the *Fitna*, except insofar as 'Ali had diminished his status as caliph by agreeing to take part in it. More important was the major split which occurred in the support for 'Ali after the battle of Siffin. On the way back to Kufa, we are told, a large part of his army withdrew their allegiance to him and left his camp because they now repented of their appeal to him to stop the fighting and enter into discussions. They demanded that 'Ali too should repent and withdraw from the arbitration. As a slogan signifying their opposition to the arbitration they adopted the formula, 'arbitration (or judgement) belongs to God alone' (*la hukma illa li'llah*), which is traditionally interpreted as a protest against the decision to appoint men (the two arbitrators) to decide what was fundamentally a religious matter and should therefore be left to God. These dissidents among the supporters of 'Ali came to be known as 'Kharijites' ('those who went out' or 'rebels') and the slogan remained a badge of the movement long after the *Fitna* was over.

For the Kharijites the immediate enemy now became 'Ali, who had to be fought until he repented of his decision to accept the arbitration. This 'Ali could not do, and from Siffin onwards he had to devote more time to his struggle against the Kharijites and less to that with Mu'awiya. He achieved a major victory over the Kharijites at the battle of Nahrawan in Iraq (658), but this, by providing the movement with martyrs, merely intensified the hatred against him.

After Siffin, therefore, we see a steady erosion of 'Ali's position: he seemed to have given grounds for the questioning of his legitimacy by agreeing to the arbitration, and the Kharijite secession threatened him on another front. At the same time the stock of Mu'awiya rose. He had come to be seen as at least an equal of 'Ali, and was able to rely on the support of his Syrian Arabs. With the collapse of 'Ali's position, we hear that the Syrians now gave their allegiance (*bay'a*) to Mu'awiya as caliph. The chronology again is not clear, but it seems to have been in 659 or 660.

After this the *Fitna* came to a dramatic end. In 661 'Ali was murdered in Kufa, reportedly by a Kharijite seeking revenge for the massacre at Nahrawan, and Mu'awiya took advantage of the situation to march into Kufa where he was able, by a combination of tact, money and the threat of force, to win the acceptance of most of 'Ali's remaining supporters. In the eyes of some of 'Ali's supporters the successor to 'Ali should have been his eldest son, Hasan, but Mu'awiya, it is generally accepted, persuaded Hasan to retract his claim to the imamate and to withdraw into private life in the Hijaz where he died some years later.[11]

Naturally, acceptance of Mu'awiya as caliph was not unanimous. He was still opposed by the Kharijites and not all of 'Ali's former supporters accepted him, but they were no longer able to carry out a consistent armed struggle against him. The remnants of 'Ali's party formed the basis of what was to become known as the Shi'a (the 'Party' of 'Ali), supporting the claims of 'Ali and his descendants to the imamate and developing into a number of sub-groups as their religious and political ideas became more elaborate. Eventually they posed a greater threat to Umayyad rule than did the Kharijites and were to play a major role in the movement which finally ended the Umayyad caliphate. This, though, was in the future. For the time being, 661 saw the end of the *Fitna*, the reunification of the divided Muslim community, and general recognition of Mu'awiya as caliph. With hindsight it was seen as the beginning of the Umayyad dynasty.

If we accept the data provided by Muslim tradition, then, the Umayyads, leading representatives of those who had opposed the Prophet until the latest possible moment, had within thirty years of his death reestablished their position to the extent that they were now at the head of the community which he had founded. As a result the *Fitna* has often been interpreted as the climax of a struggle for power within Islam between that class of Meccans typified by the Umayyads, the wealthy and powerful leaders of pre-Islamic Mecca, and those, largely from a lower social stratum, whose acceptance of Islam was more wholehearted. To use expressions frequently applied, it was the result of a struggle between the old and the new aristocracy.

Within this interpretation some have taken a more strongly anti-Umayyad line and argued that the civil war was consciously engineered by the old aristocracy in order to regain the position it had lost with the triumph of Islam. In this view Mu'awiya plays an active role by delaying answering the appeals of the caliph 'Uthman for help when he was faced with the rebellious Egyptian soldiers in Medina, arousing the Syrians by holding an exhibition in the mosque of Damascus of the dead 'Uthman's bloody shirt or severed finger, and even plotting with his relative, the keeper of 'Uthman's seal, to ensure that any possible compromise between 'Uthman and the Egyptian rebels would break down. The aim of all this was to ensure that 'Ali, whose succession to 'Uthman was seen as inevitable in any case, would succeed to the caliphate in circumstances which would cast doubt on his legitimacy and enable the old aristocracy to turn the situation to their own advantage. Others have taken a more moderate line and seen the emergence of the old aristocracy as the new leaders of Islam as an unconscious and almost inevitable process since they were the only ones with the background and skills necessary to govern and hold together the new state made possible by the Arab conquest of the Middle East. In this view Mu'awiya is the symbol of everything that the supporters of the old aristocracy wanted — a strong central government which would keep in check the unruly bedouin who had been vital for the expansion of Islam but who now threatened its survival as a unity. As the long-serving governor of a province with a tradition of ordered government dating from the Byzantine period, Mu'awiya, it is argued, was the obvious candidate of those members of the old aristocracy, whose wealth depended on trade and therefore stability, and who feared the anarchistic tendencies of the bedouin. On the other hand, 'Ali, although himself a Qurashi Meccan, had come to power on the shoulders of the discontented tribesmen and his whole campaign was bedevilled by his inability to impose discipline on his men.[12]

It may be that such interpretations accept too readily the data of Muslim tradition with its strong anti-Umayyad stance, but it nevertheless seems likely that Mu'awiya's success did owe much to the relative stability of his Syrian base and the support of the Syrian Arabs on whom he relied. Equally it appears that discontent among the tribesmen of the garrison towns had much to do with the outbreak of the *Fitna* and that 'Ali's reliance on this element was a major cause of his failure in the struggle with Mu'awiya. To this extent the interpretation of the *Fitna* as a conflict between the nomads and the developing state, between the demands of primitive democracy and those of ordered stability, is attractive. In itself, though, Mu'awiya's victory did not solve the problems which had led to the *Fitna*, and he was now faced with ruling an empire which perhaps accepted him for lack of alternatives rather than out of conviction.

Notes

1. See genealogical tables 1–3; article "Arab, Djazirat al-', part vi, in *EI2*.
2. Articles 'Ibrahim', 'Ka'ba' and 'Kuraysh' in *EI2*.

3. See genealogical tables 3–4.

4. Articles 'Umaiya b. 'Abd Shams' in *EI1*, and 'Hashim b. 'Abd Manaf' in *EI2*; Ibn Ishaq, *Sira*, English trans. A. Guillaume, *The life of Muhammad*, London 1955, 48–68; Maqrizi, *Niza'*, English trans. C. E. Bosworth, *Al-Maqrizi's 'Book of contention and strife'*.

5. H. Lammens, *Mo'âwia 1er*, Paris, 1908, 50, 171, 222, 237, 272, 394; W. M. Watt, *Muhammad at Medina*, 73–5.

6. For the attitude of Muslim tradition to the Umayyads, see above, pp. 11–18.

7. See above, pp. 3–4.

8. J. Wellhausen, *Arab kingdom*, introduction; H. A. R. Gibb, *Studies on the civilization of Islam*, 6–8, 39–44; Martin Hinds, 'Kufan political alignments and their background in the mid-seventh century A.D.', *IJMES*, 2 (1971); *idem*, 'The murder of the caliph 'Uthman', *IJMES*, 3 (1972); M. A. Shaban, *New interpretation*, 60–78.

9. Article "Othman" in *EI1*; for the suggestion that 'Uthman's 'nepotism' was merely an attempt to ensure that he could maintain control in the provinces see M. A. Shaban, *New interpretation*, 66.

10. Articles "Ali b. Abi Talib' and 'Djamal' in *EI2*.

11. Articles "Ali b. Abi Talib' and 'Adhruh' in *EI2*; J. Wellhausen, *Arab kingdom*, 75–112; H. Lammens, 'Conference de Adroh: Abou Mousa al-Aš'ari et 'Amrou ibn al-'Asi' and 'Assassinat de 'Ali. Califat ephemère de Hasan' in his *Mo'âwia 1er*; E. L. Petersen, *'Ali and Mu'awiya in early Arabic tradition*; Martin Hinds, 'The Siffin arbitration agreement', *JSS*, 17 (1972); M. A. Shaban, *New interpretation*, 60–78; G. R. Hawting, 'The significance of the slogan *la hukma illa li'llah* and the references to the *hudud* in the traditions about the Fitna and the murder of 'Uthman', *BSOAS*, 41 (1978).

12. H. A. R. Gibb, *Studies on the civilisation of Islam*, 7; N. A. Faris, 'Development in Arab historiography as reflected in the struggle between 'Ali and Mu'awiya' in B. Lewis and P. M. Holt (eds.), *Historians of the Middle East*, 435–41.

Chapter 3

The Sufyanids

Mu'awiya was the first of three caliphs from the Sufyanid branch of the Umayyad family, so called after Abu Sufyan. The Umayyad family was, indeed, very extensive and was made up of several branches often hostile to each other and competing for wealth and prestige. With the death of the Mu'awiya's grandson, the caliph Mu'awiya II, in 684, the Sufyanids were to provide no further caliphs and, as a result of the civil war which erupted even before the death of Mu'awiya II, they were supplanted in the caliphate by the Marwanid line of Umayyads descended from Marwan b. al-Hakam.[1]

After the Umayyad dynasty had been overthrown and the 'Abbasids took over the caliphate in 750, the Sufyanid branch again achieved some prominence for a time. During the first century or so of 'Abbasid rule a number of political and religious movements developed in Syria which had a strong messianic character and looked for the coming of a figure who would overthrow the 'Abbasids and reestablish Syrian glory. This figure was known as the Sufyani and was expected to be descended from the line which had produced the great Mu'awiya. It is as if the Sufyanid period of Umayyad history had come to be regarded as of special significance and something like a Golden Age for Syria.[2]

Organisation and Administration of the Caliphate[3]

From the point of view of its rulers, the major division among the peoples of the territory over which Mu'awiya had established his rule was that between the Arabs and the conquered peoples. The rapid conquest of the Middle East by the Arabs had imposed the domination of a minority elite, distinct in language, religion and way of life, over a mass of people which was itself divided by such things as language, religion, occupation and status. The *Fitna* had involved the Arabs and had only incidentally affected the conquered peoples. At the beginning of the Umayyad period it seems likely that these conquered peoples were still relatively isolated from their conquerors in everyday life and as yet largely unaffected by the processes of arabisation and islamisation which were soon to be so powerful.

The lands conquered by the Arabs and now ruled by the Umayyads were divided into provinces, each under a governor, usually at this period called the *amir*. Apart from Syria and Mesopotamia (Jazira), which came directly under the authority of the caliph, there were three other main territorial divisions within the Umayyad caliphate: Egypt and the North African territories dependent upon it; Kufa and its eastern territories; and Basra and its eastern territories. Each of these usually had an *amir* appointed directly by the caliph and this *amir* was then in turn responsible for appointing sub-governors to the towns and provinces which came under his authority. The system was not inflexible, however, and sometimes we find one *amir* acting as virtual viceroy for the whole of the east, having authority over both Kufa and Basra and all of their dependent territories, or we might find on occasion the caliph directly appointing the *amir* of a sub-province which was usually under the authority of one of the major *amirs*.

The *amir* was responsible for such things as the collection of taxes and their remission to Syria (on occasion the collection of taxes was removed from the sphere of the *amir*), the distribution of the soldiers' pay, the preservation of order, the defence of the borders and the furtherance of conquest, and the organisation and leadership of the public prayer, which had a political and communal significance and was not merely an act of worship. In effect he represented the caliph, who was at the same time religious and political leader of the Muslims, in his province.

Because of his importance, the appointment of an *amir* was one of the caliph's main concerns. In the Sufyanid period the *amir* had no independent military force at his disposal other than the tribesmen over whom he had authority, apart from a small police force (the *shurta*) which would not have been strong enough to check any major disturbance among the tribesmen. His authority over the tribesmen of his province, therefore, depended on the respect he could command and his ability to manipulate them by exploiting divisions among them. There was a tendency for the Sufyanid caliphs to appoint *amirs* from tribes like Quraysh and Thaqif which had a certain prestige among the Arabs.[4]

Below the governors, the key figures in each province were the tribal leaders, the *ashraf*, who provided the link between the governor and the tribesmen. This meant that they had to be acceptable to both parties, to the government and to the tribesmen. They owed their position among the tribesmen usually to their descent from an hereditary leading family, but as agents of the government they were appointed from above rather than below, by the governor or even the caliph, not by the tribesmen. Their position was not always a comfortable one and from time to time the *ashraf* had to come down off the fence and side either with the government or with the tribesmen. At different times they chose to descend on different sides.[5]

As can easily be imagined, the process of conquest had disrupted the tribal situation which had existed in pre-Islamic Arabia. Tribes had been removed from their homelands, fragmented, and resettled sometimes in a number of areas remote from one another, and in contact with other tribes, which had gone through the same process. Tribes which before had been strong and important might now be poorly represented in a given area in the conquered lands and forced into alliance with other tribes with which they had previously had little contact. The result was both a reconstruction and intensification of the tribal system of pre-Islamic Arabia, and a reformulation of the genealogical links which were its mythological justification. Probably the most notable example of this reformulation of genealogy was the case of the tribe of Quda'a which dominated central Syria. As a result of the second civil war at the end of the Sufyanid period, Quda'a, who had previously been regarded as 'northerners' (descendants of Isma'il), became 'southerners' (descendants of Qahtan) for the simple reason that most of their opponents in Syria were 'northerners' and Quda'a found it necessary to obtain the support of the 'southerners' there.

The development of the large tribal confederations, culminating in the polarisation of all the Arabs between the two groups of 'northerners' and 'southerners', therefore, was the result of specific social, economic and political conditions and events in the period following the Arab conquest of the Middle East. It was not, as is often assumed, something which the Arabs brought with them out of pre-Islamic Arabia. In pre-Islamic Arabia, certainly, there were feuds and alliances involving more than one tribe, but they were relatively limited and localised, not involving all of the Arabs nor covering all of Arabia. The first indication that we have of the new, more intensified and widespread formation of supra-tribal groups among the Arabs is at the time of the second civil war, almost simultaneously in Syria and Iraq. It obviously has to be explained by such things as the disruption of the old way of life, the need to forge new social links in the post-conquest conditions, and the struggle for land and resources among the Arabs, intensified when new groups of Arab immigrants moved into an area and challenged the position of those already settled there. With the breakdown of Umayyad authority at the end of the Sufyanid period the lid was removed from a mixture which had been fermenting for some time.[6]

The other, larger population which the caliphs and their governors ruled was that of the conquered peoples, and, just as the Arabs were governed indirectly by means of their tribal notables, so the non-Arabs were generally administered through their own native authorities, priests, rabbis, nobles or others. At this early date it seems that little assimilation or even contact between conquerors and conquered was envisaged, and the latter were regarded by their rulers mainly as a source of revenue for the benefit of the Arabs. The nature of the taxes imposed on the conquered peoples is still, in spite of much scholarly debate, rather obscure and probably varied from place to place according to, first, the way in which the locality was conquered by the Arabs — by force or by agreement — and, secondly, the nature of the taxation system which had existed in the locality before its conquest. Nevertheless, at the taxpayer's level it seems likely that there was generally a dual system of poll tax (i.e., a tax levied at a fixed rate on individual persons) and land tax and that the poll tax was a sign of social or religious inferiority. There was as yet probably no fixed and universally used terminology for the various taxes, and, as far as the Arabs are concerned, they probably only interested themselves to the extent of making sure that the non-Arab notables handed over the required sums. How these notables raised the sums from the non-Arab communities did not concern the Arabs.

Even in the short term the effects of the Arab conquest on the non-Arab people of the Middle East must have been considerable, but our Arabic sources only supply incidental information on this issue and it is only quite recently that detailed study of this question, involving the use of a range of sources produced in various languages, has begun. Some of the effects of the conquest on the non-Arab peoples are fairly obvious, such things as the virtual disappearance of the former Byzantine and Sasanid ruling classes, and the demographic redistribution brought about by war and captivity and the foundation of new major settlements like Basra and Kufa. Other suggested consequences — regarding, for instance, the strengthening or weakening of Monophysite and Nestorian Christianity, or the transformation of the Jews from an agricultural to a predominantly urban and mercantile people — are more debatable.[7]

Of the lands ruled by the Umayyads, Syria, the centre of Umayyad power, was neither the richest nor most populous, but owed its importance to a number of other factors. The long and continuous association with Mu'awiya before he became caliph, and the fact that he was able to call on the support of one strong tribal group in Syria, Quda'a, in contrast to the multiplicity of tribal fragments elsewhere, have already been mentioned. In Syria too the fact that the Arabs settled among the local population, in already existing towns such as Damascus and Hims, seems to indicate a certain security in comparison with Iraq and Egypt where new garrison towns were founded and the Arabs kept apart from the local population. Furthermore, Syria, although it was the centre of the Umayyad territories, had a border with Byzantium and this meant that the Syrian Arabs could be kept active in warfare against the infidel without having to send them to far distant borders. Finally, the religious significance of Syria, and particularly of Jerusalem, may have been greater for nascent Islam than it was at a later period.

For military and administrative purposes, Syria was at first divided into four districts or *ajnad*: Damascus, Hims, Jordan with its centre at Tiberias, and Palestine with its centre at Ramla. Later, about 680, a fifth district was added, Qinnasrin in the north, probably in connection with the warfare against Byzantium. From one point of view, the Umayyad period can be characterised as a brief and fairly unusual time of Syrian domination of the Middle East.

Of the other provinces, Iraq was the richest and most valuable. Benefiting from the climate and fertility of the lower Tigris and Euphrates valleys, the agricultural land was given a name indicative of its richness: it was the *sawad*, the black land. Iraq was also the military centre from which the lands to the east were conquered and administered, and its garrison towns of Kufa and Basra provided the Arab settlers for the eastern provinces. Like Syria, Kufa and Basra were subdivided for military and administrative purposes. Kufa had originally been divided into sevenths, but around 670 was reorganised into quarters. Basra was divided into fifths. Each of these subdivisions consisted of a number of tribal groups, and it has been argued that the less volatile character of Basra, as compared to Kufa, may be partly explained by the less heterogeneous nature of the tribal groupings in the Basran divisions compared with those in Kufa. The reorganisation of Kufa into quarters may have been intended to decrease the fragmentation of the sevenths. The importance of Iraq for the development of Islam during the Umayyad period meant that its influence was decisive too for the formation of the historical tradition for the period. Our sources tend to reflect the viewpoint of Iraq, with its anti-Umayyad point of view, and provide us with more information about events in Iraq and the east than in the other provinces.

Khurasan, the north-east border province of the Umayyads, was the most important eastern dependency of Iraq so far as the history of the Umayyad period is concerned. The early Umayyad period saw its conquest and settlement by the Arabs, and it then served as a base for expansion and raids further east. Its two chief towns were both garrison centres, Nishapur in the west of the province and Merv in the east. To some extent the tensions among the Arabs of Iraq were carried over into Khurasan, where they were able to intensify away from the close control of the Umayyad government. They were made more dangerous for the government because the Arabs of Khurasan, unlike those of Iraq, continued to be involved in constant military activity, and they were altered by the different society which existed in the province. It was there that the movement which eventually overthrew the Umayyads became strong.

Finally, although we do not hear nearly so much about Egypt under the Umayyads, it too was extremely important militarily and economically. Its fertility depending on the annual rise and fall of the Nile, Egypt was the granary of the Mediterranean, and from it the infertile but religiously important region of the Hijaz was supplied with food. It was from Egypt that North Africa was conquered and settled. It is also important to remember that, although our Muslim literary sources are relatively uninformative about Egypt during this period, it is virtually the only region for which we have a substantial body of contemporary administrative material, preserved on papyrus, enabling us to put together a more certain picture of the Umayyad administration than is possible for the other provinces.[8]

Events and Personalities of the Sufyanid Period[9]

Mu'awiya (caliph 661–80) was succeeded by his son Yazid (680–3) and his grandson, Mu'awiya II, son of Yazid, whose caliphate of brief duration and limited authority lasted at most a few months at the end of 683 and the beginning of 684. However, reflecting the predominance of Iraq in the formation of Muslim tradition, we hear rather more about the governors of Iraq throughout the Umayyad period than we do about the caliphs in Syria. Three Iraqi governors under the Sufyanids are prominent: Mughira b. Shu'ba, governor of Kufa, died in about 670; after him Ziyad governed the whole of Iraq from Basra until his death in about 673; and finally Ziyad's son, 'Ubayd Allah, succeeded to his father's office in 675 and remained there under the remainder of Mu'awiya's caliphate and that of Yazid until he was finally driven out in the second civil war. All three of these Iraqi governors were Thaqafis, members of the tribe of Thaqif from the town of Ta'if in the Hijaz south-east of Mecca. In the pre-Islamic period Thaqif were allies of Quraysh and in the Umayyad period they provided a number of provincial governors.

Mughira is portrayed as a disreputable individual, guilty of murder and adultery, who nevertheless was able to push himself forward by ingratiating himself with movements (like Islam) or men (like Mu'awiya) in the ascendant. In the *Fitna* he had thrown in his lot with Mu'awiya and been appointed governor of Kufa after Mu'awiya's victory over 'Ali. As governor, he acquired the reputation of someone who was more concerned to avoid than to deal with trouble, taking little positive action himself and leaving his successors to face the consequences.[10]

According to tradition, Ziyad's father was unknown, his mother having been a prostitute in Ta'if. Hence he is often known as Ziyad b. Abihi, Ziyad the son of his father. Settling in Basra at an early date, Ziyad had supported 'Ali in the *Fitna* and the latter had made him his governor of Fars, the province of south-west Persia. After Mu'awiya's victory, Ziyad had been persuaded by his Thaqafi relative Mughira to come over to the victor, and material incentives were, of course, important. The importance attached by Mu'awiya to the support of Ziyad is shown by the fact that the caliph went so far as to acknowledge the Thaqafi as his own half-brother by publicly stating that Abu Sufyan was in fact Ziyad's father too. Hence the latter is sometimes referred to as Ziyad b. Abi Sufyan. In effect Ziyad was thus made a member of the Umayyad family. The whole affair (known as *al-istilhaq*) is rather obscure and has an aura of scandal around it, and Ziyad does not seem to have been exactly welcomed by the other Sufyanids.

About 665 Mu'awiya appointed Ziyad over Basra under the control of Mughira in Kufa. His arrival in the garrison town was the occasion of a famous introductory speech (*khutba*) in the mosque in which he warned the Basrans of his determination to impose order: 'We have brought a punishment to fit every crime. Whoever drowns another will himself be drowned; whoever burns another will be burned; whoever breaks into a house, I will break into his heart; and whoever breaks open a grave, I will bury him alive in it.' On the death of Mughira, about five years later, Ziyad succeeded him as viceroy of the east.

Apart from his reorganisation of Kufa into quarters and his decision to undertake the settlement of Iraqis in Khurasan, which may also be explained as a measure to defuse possibly dangerous developments in Iraq, Ziyad's governorship is associated with the suppression of the revolt of Hujr b. 'Adi in Kufa in 671. This was significant since Hujr's revolt was the first movement openly in support of the claims of the descendants of 'Ali since the end of the *Fitna* and was a harbinger of things to come. In itself it did not prove difficult to suppress. Ziyad was able to isolate Hujr and certain other ringleaders from the Kufan soldiers who had initially supported him, and Hujr and six others were sent to Damascus where Mu'awiya had them executed. Kufa was to become the centre of Shi'ite opposition to the Umayyads and the scene of a number of anti-Umayyad movements but, as in the case of Hujr b. 'Adi, there was a tendency for the Kufans to back down after initially encouraging the outbreak of revolt, leaving the leaders and those members of the house of 'Ali on whose behalf the revolt had been planned high and dry. Kufa's pro-Shi'ite reputation, therefore, is to some extent double-edged and tinged with guilt.[11]

The third of the important governors of Iraq for the Sufyanids, 'Ubayd Allah b. Ziyad, became especially prominent after the death of Mu'awiya, and his role in events will be discussed in connection with the second civil war.

Regarding the caliph Mu'awiya in Syria, the period of his rule is portrayed as one of internal security and external expansion and aggression. In Syria he had close ties with the Quda'a, led by the tribe of Kalb, members of whom were prominent in his retinue and from whom he took a wife, the mother of his son Yazid. Certain details indicate too that he was respectful of the traditions of his Christian subjects who still must have been the majority in the Syrian towns. One of his officials and advisors was Sarjun (Sergius), a member of a Greek Orthodox family which had served the Byzantine administration of Damascus, and father of the important Orthodox theologian, St John of Damascus (d. about 748). Respect for the Christians of Syria, though, does not appear to have inhibited Mu'awiya's military activity against the Byzantines. In the Aegean, Rhodes and Crete were occupied, and between 674 and 680 a series of attacks were made on Constantinople from a base in the sea of Marmara. In North Africa Qayrawan was founded in 670 as a base for further penetration, and in the east, where Ziyad was instrumental in organising the occupation of Khurasan, major cities like Kabul, Bukhara and Samarqand are said to have submitted to the Arabs for the first time.

In tradition Mu'awiya's image is somewhat two-sided. On the one hand he is regarded as a clever and successful ruler who got what he wanted by persuasion rather than force. The key concept here is that of *hilm*. This is a traditional Arab virtue signifying subtlety and cunning in the management of men and affairs and it is seen as a desideratum for the traditional Arab leader. Mu'awiya is traditionally portrayed as one of the supreme exemplars of the virtue of *hilm*, using flattery and material inducements rather than force, ruling in the style of a tribal shaykh who has no coercive power at his disposal and depends upon his own reputation and persuasive skills. Muslim tradition credits him with a succinct summary of his political philosophy: 'I never use my voice if I can use my money, never my whip if I can use my voice, never my sword if I can use my whip; but, if I have to use my sword, I will.' To some extent this image of Mu'awiya is reflected in non-Muslim historical tradition, for the Greek chronicler Theophanes (d. 818) refers to Mu'awiya as *protosymboulos*, that is, first among equals, and thus implicitly makes a contrast with the more usual type of state ruler of the time. It seems likely that Mu'awiya encouraged this image. One of the Syriac writers of the time notes that he did not wear a crown like other rulers of the world, and one of the recurrent institutions about which we hear in connection with Mu'awiya's rule is that of the *wafd* or delegation. This is a reference to his practice of inviting the leaders of the Arabs in the provinces to come to his court in Syria where he flattered them and treated them well before sending them back to their province with suitable presents, having persuaded them of the merits of a plan which he had in mind and which they in turn were to recommend to the Arabs in their province. Of course, it is not surprising that Mu'awiya should attempt to portray himself, particularly to his Arab subjects, as fundamentally a tribal shaykh, but we should not be misled into forgetting that his power and resources were far greater than those available to a pre-Islamic Arab tribal leader and, in addition, that the caliphate was not merely a political office but a religious one at the same time.

The other image of Mu'awiya in tradition is to some extent at variance with this portrait of him as a successor to the authority of a tribal shaykh. He is the man who perverted the caliphate into a kingship, the first to make the *khilafa* a *mulk*. The significance of this contrast between caliphate and kingship and of the charge that the Umayyads were not caliphs but merely kings has already been discussed. In connection with Mu'awiya the charge centres on his decision to appoint his son Yazid as his successor (*wali 'l-'ahd*) while he himself was still alive and in possession of the caliphate. The reports about how Mu'awiya went about this — his careful planning, his secrecy while preparing the ground, his reception of the delegations from the provinces and his winning their support for his plan, the pressure put on Yazid to change his way of life in order to make him acceptable as a successor — are perhaps the best illustration of the *hilm* of Mu'awiya, and it seems that he was successful in that the move does not appear to have called forth any opposition from the tribesmen in the provinces. What opposition there was came from a relatively small group of people who may have considered that they had claims to the caliphate, and in tradition these individuals tend to appear as spokesmen of Islam against Mu'awiya's attempt to introduce dynastic rule into the Muslim community. How important this consideration was at the time is not easy to say, but it is clear that the opposition of tradition to Mu'awiya is based on religious as much as political principles. It is not a protest of primitive tribal democracy at the growth of Umayyad power but rather a protest of Islam at what was seen as Umayyad disregard of Muslim norms (which cannot have existed in any developed sense in the time of Mu'awiya). At any rate, the second civil war is seen as a direct consequence of Mu'awiya's action.

It is indicative of the somewhat contradictory image of Mu'awiya that it is reported that when he died in 680 he was buried with hair and nail clippings from the Prophet himself, thus emphasising that Mu'awiya had been a companion of Muhammad, having acquired these relics when he acted as the Prophet's secretary. On the whole it is notable that the Umayyads do not seem to have emphasised their succession from the Prophet, unlike the 'Abbasids who used alleged relics of the Prophet — notably his cloak — as part of their regalia. Mu'awiya was succeeded, as he had planned, by his son Yazid, but Yazid was faced with a series of movements of opposition and when he himself died towards the end of 683 Sufyanid rule in effect collapsed.[12]

Notes

1. See genealogical tables 1, 3 and 4.
2. H. Lammens, 'Le "Sofiani", héros national des arabes syriens' in his *Etudes sur le siècle des omayyades*; P. K. Hitti, *History of Syria*, 540–1; F. Omar, *The 'Abbasid caliphate*, 268 ff.; K. Salibi, *Syria under Islam*, 38–42.
3. There is no general work devoted to the administration and organisation of the Umayyad state. See, however, the articles "Amil', 'Amir', "Arif', 'Diwan', etc, in *EI1* and *EI2*. For a concise analysis of the way in which the state was run in the Sufyanid period see P. Crone, *Slaves on Horses*, 29–33.
4. Articles 'Amir' and "Amil' in *EI2*; J. Wellhausen, *Arab kingdom, passim*.
5. Article 'Sharif' in *EI1*; P. Crone, *Slaves on Horses*, 31–2.
6. I. Goldziher, *Muslim Studies*, i, 87 ff.; L. Massignon, 'Explication du plan de Kufa', *Melanges Maspero*, Cairo 1934–40; *idem*, 'Explication du plan de Basra', *Westöstliche Abhandlungen R. Tschudi*, ed. F. Meier, Wiesbaden 1954; C. Pellat, *Le milieu basrien et la formation de Gahiz*; F. McGraw Donner, *The early Islamic conquests*, 226–50; M. Morony, *Iraq after the Muslim conquest*, 236–53.
7. M. Morony, *Iraq after the Muslim conquest*, 167–235, 265–74; D. C. Dennett, *Conversion and the poll tax in early Islam, passim*, for the agreements made from region to region at the time of the conquests; M. A. Cook and P. Crone, *Hagarism*, 83–106.
8. On Egypt under the Umayyads: H. I. Bell, 'The administration of Egypt under the Umayyad Khalifs', *BZ*, 28 (1928); H. Lammens, 'Un gouverneur omayyade d'Egypte, Qorra ibn Šarik', *Etudes sur le siècle des Omayyades*. On Syria: P. K. Hitti, *History of Syria*; K. Salibi, *Syria under Islam*. On Iraq: M. Morony, *Iraq after the Muslim conquest*. On Khurasan: J. Wellhausen, *Arab kingdom*, 397 ff.;' M. A. Shaban, 'Khurasan at the time of the Arab conquest' in *Iran and Islam*, ed. C. E. Bosworth, 479–90. For an attempt to rank the provinces in order of economic importance, Gernot Rotter, *Die Umayyaden und der zweite Bürgerkrieg*, 60 ff.
9. In addition to the specific references given below, reference should be made to the indices and bibliographies of more general books on the Umayyad period and Islam, in particular: M. A. Shaban, *New interpretation*, M. G. Hodgson, *The venture of Islam*, P. Crone, *Slaves on horses*, M. Morony, *Iraq after the Muslim conquest*, and vol iv of *The Cambridge history of Iran*.
10. Article 'al-Mughira b. Shu'ba' in *EI1*; J. Wellhausen, *Arab kingdom*, 114–18;

H. Lammens, *Mu'âwia 1er*, *passim*, and *Le siècle des Omayyades*, 28–41.
11. Article 'Ziyad b. Abihi' in *EI1*; J. Wellhausen, *Arab kingdom*, 119–30; H. Lammens, 'Ziad b. Abihi, vice-roi de l'Iraq, lieutenant de Mo'âwia I', *Le siècle des Omayyades*; K. Fariq, 'A remarkable early Muslim governor, Ziyad ibn Abih', *IC*, 26 (1952); *idem, Ziyad b. Abih*, London 1966; article 'Hudjr b. 'Adi' in *EI2*; J. Wellhausen, *The religio-political factions*, 95–103; W. M. Watt, 'Shi'ism under the Umayyads', *JRAS* (1960); S. M. Jafri, *Origins and early development of Shi'a Islam*, 159–66; M. Morony, *Iraq after the Muslim conquest*, 486–7.
12. J. Wellhausen, *Arab kingdom*, 131–45; H. Lammens, *Mo'âwia 1er*; I. Goldziher, 'Mu'awija I, der Begründer des Islamstaates', in his *Gesammelte Schriften*, v, 164–7; M. A. J. Beg, 'Mu'awiya: a critical survey', *IC*, 51 (1977).

Chapter 4

The Second Civil War

The second civil war[1] is sometimes called the *fitna* of Ibn al-Zubayr because the struggle between the Umayyads and Ibn al-Zubayr is the main theme which runs through it from its gradual beginnings during the caliphate of Yazid b. Mu'awiya until its conclusion with the death of Ibn al-Zubayr probably in 692. It contains, however, a number of other events or episodes which are only loosely connected with each other and with the struggle between the Umayyads and Ibn al-Zubayr. Put in a general way, tensions and pressures which had been suppressed by Mu'awiya came to the surface during Yazid's caliphate and erupted after his death, when Umayyad authority was temporarily eclipsed. With the reestablishment of the line of Umayyad caliphs, in the persons of Marwan (684–5) and his son 'Abd al-Malik (685–705), Umayyad authority was gradually reimposed.

The two fundamental facts which provided the immediate opportunity for the outbreak of the second civil war were, firstly, the refusal of certain leading Muslims to accept Yazid as caliph and, secondly, the failure of the Sufyanids to supply suitable candidates for the caliphate after the death of Yazid.

Firstly, as we have seen, Mu'awiya's attempt to secure, during his own lifetime, recognition of his son Yazid as his successor, although not opposed by the Arab tribesmen, was rejected by a small group of prominent Muslims. They were all members of Quraysh with some claim to be considered as caliphal candidates themselves, and they were all resident in Medina. For our purposes, the two most important of them are 'Abd Allah b. al-Zubayr, son of a leading companion of Muhammad who had been killed after fighting against 'Ali at the battle of the Camel in the first civil war, and Husayn b. 'Ali, grandson of the Prophet Muhammad and leader of the descendants of 'Ali after the death of his elder brother Hasan who had not pursued his own claims to the imamate after Mu'awiya's victory over 'Ali. When Yazid succeeded Mu'awiya in

46

680 he made renewed attempts to secure recognition from these men, but Ibn al-Zubayr and Husayn eluded the Umayyad governor of Medina and fled to Mecca.[2]

Secondly, the Sufyanid line petered out after the death of Yazid in 683. Yazid was succeeded by his son Mu'awiya II, but the latter never enjoyed much authority and may have been rejected outside central and southern Syria. Some reports talk of his ill health, others stress his comparative youthfulness, and in any case he survived his father only by a few months. Although the chronology of the period is quite obscure, it seems likely that many former supporters of the Umayyads had already decided to seek a caliph elsewhere even while Mu'awiya II still lived. Other possibilities from among the Sufyanid branch were deemed unsuitable, and eventually those who still supported the Umayyads turned to Marwan of the Abu 'l-'As branch of the family, although the choice may not have been as obvious as his descendants tried to portray it. It was the doubts about the continuation of Umayyad rule, associated with the failure of the Sufyanid line, which enabled the various religious, political and tribal tensions to develop into civil war.[3]

The main theme of this civil war, then, was the attempt by 'Abd Allah b. al-Zubayr to establish himself as caliph or commander of the faithful, and the subsequent struggle for supremacy between him and the Umayyads. Although he refused to accept Yazid as caliph, tradition has it that Ibn al-Zubayr did not in fact put himself forward for the office until after Yazid's death. Before that event he merely remained in Mecca, calling himself 'the fugitive at the sanctuary' (*al-'a'idh bi'l-bayt*), denouncing Yazid and joining with other opposition groups against Yazid. After the failure at Karbala' in 680 of Husayn's attempted revolt, which will be discussed shortly, there were two opposition movements in particular which were in contact with Ibn al-Zubayr. One was a revolt of the people of Medina, who had publicly withdrawn their allegiance to Yazid, in spite of his attempts to conciliate their leaders, in reaction, we are told, to the caliph's personal unsuitability for his office — charges such as enjoyment of singing girls and playing with a pet monkey are brought against him in the tradition. The other opposition movement involved Kharijites, apparently from both Basra and parts of Arabia. Towards the end of his life, in 683, Yazid raised an army to go to the Hijaz, with the aim of crushing both the Medinese opposition and that of Ibn al-Zubayr. The commander was a Syrian Arab of the 'northern' confederation of Qays, Muslim b. 'Uqba al-

Murri. This army defeated the Medinese at the battle of the Harra (summer 683) and subsequently occupied the town, allegedly plundering it and exacting oaths of allegiance to Yazid from the Medinese. This sack of the town of the Prophet, which Muslims come to see as the home of the *Sunna*, is one of the major crimes charged against the Umayyads in tradition.[4]

Having subdued Medina, the army continued to Mecca but Muslim b. 'Uqba died on the way and command was taken over by Husayn b. Numayr al-Sakuni. When Husayn reached Mecca, and Ibn al-Zubayr refused to submit, a siege of the town was begun and catapults erected to bombard it. At some stage in the course of the siege the Ka'ba caught fire and was badly damaged. The circumstances are quite obscure but, as one might expect, there is a tendency in the sources to attach blame to the besieging army, and this siege and bombardment too figure prominently in the lists of Umayyad crimes. Before the siege could be brought to a successful conclusion, however, news reached the Syrians of the death of the caliph Yazid in November 683, upon which Husayn b. Numayr entered into negotiations with Ibn al-Zubayr. It is reported that Husayn offered to recognise Ibn al-Zubayr as caliph if he would leave Mecca and return with the army to Syria. This, however, Ibn al-Zubayr refused and consequently the Syrian army returned home, leaving him in control of Mecca.[5]

After the death of Yazid, although events in Syria are rather obscure, it is clear that Umayyad authority collapsed almost everywhere and Ibn al-Zubayr was able to extend his authority over most of the Arab lands, eventually appointing his brother Mus'ab b. al-Zubayr to be governor of Iraq. The extent of Ibn al-Zubayr's authority is attested by coins bearing his name from the Persian provinces of Fars and Kirman. Even in Syria the 'northern' confederacy of Qays recognised his caliphate. At this point he was, in fact, the generally recognised caliph of the Muslims, Umayyad authority being limited to central and southern Syria. Once the hiatus in the Umayyad line had been closed with the accession of Marwan to the caliphate in 684, however, Zubayrid authority began to be pushed back. A start was made already by Marwan, who recaptured Egypt for the Umayyads during his nine-month tenure of power (he died in 685). The final Umayyad victory came under the caliphate of his son 'Abd al-Malik (685–705), partly as a result of the political and military measures which he undertook, but in large measure because of Ibn al-Zubayr's inability to maintain firm control of those areas, notably Iraq, which had initially recognised him. In 691 'Abd al-Malik was able to march into Iraq, defeating and killing Ibn al-Zubayr's governor Mus'ab, and following this he sent an army under the command of al-Hajjaj against Ibn al-Zubayr in Mecca. The second siege of Mecca, by al-Hajjaj, is reported in terms very similar to the earlier siege led by Husayn b. Numayr. Again catapults were erected and the town bombarded. This time, though, the siege was pressed home and eventually, probably in November 692, Mecca fell, and Ibn al-Zubayr, now aged about 70 (he had been the first child born to those who had made the *hijra* to Medina with Muhammad in 622), fell in the final attack.[6]

This marked the end of the second civil war. Ibn al-Zubayr does not seem to have espoused any distinctive religious or political programme in the manner of the Shi'ites and the Kharijites (we are told that his alliance with the Kharijites foundered when he refused to accept their religious and political programme), and it seems that he won support mainly because of his status as one of the first generation of Muslims and a member of Quraysh at a time when the Umayyads were weak and opposition to them strong in different quarters. One thing that is notable, however, is the strong association between him and the Muslim sanctuary at Mecca. We have seen that he fled to Mecca, called himself *al-'a'idh bi'l-bayt*, and refused to leave it when offered the caliphate by Husayn b. Numayr. In the traditions the Umayyads often refer to him as 'the evil-doer (*mulhid*) at Mecca'. After the end of the first siege, we are told, he rebuilt the Ka'ba and made some significant changes to its form, citing the authority of the Prophet for them. When al-Hajjaj had killed Ibn al-Zubayr and recaptured Mecca, the Umayyad commander destroyed the changes which had been made by Ibn al-Zubayr and restored the Ka'ba to the form it had had before. While the struggle with Ibn al-Zubayr was at its height, 'Abd al-Malik undertook the construction of the unique sanctuary of the Dome of the Rock in Jerusalem. The interpretation of these developments is certainly debatable and to some extent obscure, but one may suggest that an argument about the sanctuary, its nature and its site, was an important element in the conflict between Ibn al-Zubayr and the Umayyads.[7]

Apart from Ibn al-Zubayr, the second civil war also saw attempts to gain power by, or on behalf of, descendants of 'Ali and although they had only limited success, in the longer term they turned out to be very important.

While Yazid was still alive and Ibn al-Zubayr had not yet put himself forward as caliph, Husayn, the son of 'Ali and the Prophet Muhammad's daughter Fatima, was persuaded to make a bid for power. Since the death of his brother Hasan, he was the most prominent of 'Ali's children and, as we have seen, was one of those who refused to accept the caliphate of Yazid. In 680, after fleeing together with Ibn al-Zubayr from Medina to Mecca, he was told that he could expect to receive substantial support in Kufa, his father's former headquarters and already scene of the abortive revolt of Hujr b. 'Adi, if he would only go there. Thus encouraged, he set out, but the Umayyad authorities got wind of what was going on. Husayn and his small band of followers were never allowed to get into Kufa but were surrounded at Karbala' in the desert to the north of the garrison town where they were all killed after fighting broke out. Seventy heads, including that of Husayn, are said to have been displayed in Kufa afterwards, and Husayn's was then forwarded to Damascus where Yazid had it put up for show. The Umayyad governor of Iraq at the time was 'Ubayd Allah b. Ziyad and he, in particular, is associated in tradition with the suppression of Husayn's movement, although the bloodshed is often ascribed to others. The date of the fight at Karbala' was, according to the Muslim *hijri* calendar, 10 Muharram 61 (10 October 680).[8]

The event has attained a mythic quality in Muslim, and especially Shi'ite, tradition. For the Shi'a Karbala' is the supreme example of the pattern of suffering and martyrdom which has afflicted their imams and the whole of the Shi'ite community. Each year the day of Karbala', 10 Muharram, is marked by Shi'ites as their greatest festival, and the passion plays and flagellants' processions which accompany it illustrate the feeling which memory of the event inspires. It is only to be expected, therefore, that it is virtually impossible to disentangle history from the legend and hagiography with which it is associated. Even Sunni Muslims are moved by the fate of the Prophet's grandson.[9] It seems unlikely that at the time itself the affair had very much importance for the Umayyads. Husayn's force had been small and was suppressed with relative ease. If there was a worry, it was more on account of the disturbances which had occurred in Kufa prior to the arrival of Husayn in Iraq, disturbances which had caused 'Ubayd Allah b. Ziyad to be shut up in the citadel of Kufa for a while, and which illustrated the continuing instability and sympathy for the 'Alids in this important garrison town. It is, therefore, in the long run, in its emotive and mythological significance, that Karbala' is really important. In a negative way, however, it also had some importance: it meant that when Umayyad authority faltered after the death of Yazid, the descendants of 'Ali and Fatima, many of whom had died along with Husayn, were in no position to take advantage of the situation.

There was, however, another line of descent from 'Ali, and it was on behalf of a representative of this line that the second major 'Alid movement of the second civil war developed. This was the revolt led by Mukhtar (a Thaqafi) on behalf of Muhammad b. al-Hanafiyya, son of 'Ali by a wife known as the Hanafi woman. This revolt, also centred on Kufa, occurred between 685 and 687. By this time Iraq had come under the authority of Ibn al-Zubayr and the revolt of Mukhtar was directed in the first instance against the Zubayrids rather than the Umayyads. Mukhtar himself is portrayed as an ambitious adventurer (the sources are all hostile to him) who was able to take advantage of the conditions in Kufa following the death of Husayn to establish a temporary supremacy there and in the territories dependent upon it. His revolt was preceded by a movement known as that of the Penitents (*al-tawwabun*), Kufans who, aroused by feelings of guilt over their lack of support for Husayn, sacrificed themselves in a futile battle against the Umayyads in Mesopotamia. How far Mukhtar really had the support of the man in whose name he claimed to be acting, Muhammad b. al-Hanafiyya, is questionable, but he seems to have been able to persuade many Kufans that he was his agent. Mukhtar's movement is interesting and important in a number of ways.

In the first place, this is the first time that the *mawali* are shown to play a significant part in events. In modern writing on the Umayyad period the relative importance of Arabs and *mawali* in certain episodes has become a topic of debate and argument. Older writers may have overemphasised the role of the *mawali* and in reaction some more modern writers have stressed the importance, indeed the leading role, of the Arabs. Nevertheless, nearly all the sources, and in particular a contemporary non-Muslim source, agree that non-Arabs were prominent and numerous among the supporters of Mukhtar. Indeed, Mukhtar formed a personal bodyguard (*haras*) from the *mawali*, commanded by one of their number, Abu 'Amr Kaysan. The followers of Mukhtar are often referred to generally as the 'Kaysaniyya'. At this time, by the term *mawali* we are mainly referring to prisoners of war and their descendants, brought to Kufa in the wake of the upheavals of the Arab conquests, and not the peasant fugitives of a slightly later date. Nevertheless, Mukhtar could not rely on non-Arab support alone and he had to win the support too of the *ashraf* of Kufa. In this he had some success, but the relationship between Mukhtar and the Arabs seems to have been an uneasy one. Towards the end of the period of his dominance in Kufa many of the *ashraf* rebelled against him, we are told because of his too favourable attitude to the *mawali*, and after he had suppressed the revolt many of the *ashraf* fled to Basra which was still in Zubayrid hands.

Secondly, Mukhtar's movement is of religious interest, although the significance of some of the information we have about this aspect of it is unclear. Generally his movement is shown to have been coloured by religious ideas and practices of non-Arab and non-Islamic origin and dubious legitimacy. One of the most striking instances is the practice ascribed to his followers of carrying a chair which they called the chair of 'Ali and which they took into battle and walked around like the Hebrew Ark of the Covenant. It is in connection with Mukhtar's movement too that the idea of the *mahdi*, the messianic figure who is expected at the end of time to restore the world to a state of justice and righteousness, occurs apparently for the first time. He is said to have proclaimed Ibn al-Hanafiyya as the *mahdi* while he himself was his *wazir*, or helper. The idea of the *mahdi* was to become characteristic of Islam, especially in its Shi'ite forms, but it is not attested before the time of Mukhtar. The appearance of ideas like these in Mukhtar's movement has sometimes been connected with the importance of the *mawali* in his following, the suggestion being that these non-Arabs brought with them into Islam religious concepts derived from their pre-Islamic backgrounds, such as the idea of the messiah or that of the transmigration of souls. These concepts would then have been grafted on to what was an original pure Arab Islam. The difficulty, of course, would lie in isolating the content of this alleged pure form of Islam before it became 'contaminated' by foreign 'borrowings'.

Thirdly, Mukhtar's movement looks to the future. There seems to be a thread running from Mukhtar to the movement which eventually overthrew the Umayyads, that of the Hashimiyya. The crushing of Mukhtar's revolt did not, it seems, end support for Ibn al-Hanafiyya as the rightful imam, and when he too died some of his followers transferred their hopes to his son Abu Hashim. This Abu Hashim then, according to early 'Abbasid tradition, transferred on his deathbed his rights to the imamate to the 'Abbasid family. Thus the 'Abbasids claimed to be the rightful leaders of the movement which had originally supported Muhammad b. al-Hanafiyya, and this seems to have been one of the 'Abbasids' main claims to legitimacy in the early part of their caliphate. From one point of view, therefore, the triumph of the Hashimiyya in 749 and 750 can be seen as the ultimate victory of the movement which had begun with Mukhtar's revolt. It was only after the accession of the 'Abbasids that the line of descent from 'Ali and Fatima again became the main focus of Shi'ite hopes.

Eventually, in the spring of 687, Mukhtar's revolt was crushed by the Zubayrid governor of Basra with the support of those Kufan *ashraf* who had fled from Mukhtar's rule. Before that happened, however, he, or rather his general, the Arab Ibrahim al-Ashtar, whose father had been one of 'Ali's chief supporters, had achieved a striking victory over the Umayyads. That was in the summer of 686 at the battle on the river Khazir near Mosul. The Umayyad army was led by 'Ubayd Allah b. Ziyad, who, after being driven out of Iraq in the period following the death of Yazid, had made his way to Syria and given his support to the Marwanids. 'Abd al-Malik now sent him to restore Umayyad authority in Mesopotamia, but his defeat and death at the hands of Mukhtar's men meant that 'Abd al-Malik had to postpone his planned reconquest of Iraq for some years more. The death of 'Ubayd Allah in this battle at the hands of the supporters of Mukhtar came to be portrayed as justice for his involvement in the events of Karbala'. One of Mukhtar's slogans had demanded vengeance for Husayn and the battle on the Khazir was seen as obtaining it. Some sources go so far as to say that 'Ubayd Allah, like Husayn, was killed on the 10 Muharram, but a different day of the month seems more likely.[10]

In addition to the attempts by Zubayrids and Shi'ites to overthrow the established order, the final theme of the second civil war is the development of polarised factionalism among the Arab tribesmen. For the first time we hear of the appearance among the Arab tribes of two extensive and mutually hostile alliances, based generally on the 'northern' and 'southern' genealogical groupings. This occurs at almost the same time in Syria and in Basra, and the immediate cause in each case was the crisis in Umayyad authority which encouraged discontented elements to look for better fortunes under non-Umayyad leaders.

In Syria, the factionalism developed around, on the one side, the

Quda'a, led by the tribe of Kalb, and on the other the confederation of Qays. Quda'a were strong in the central and southern regions of Syria, while Qays predominated in the north and in Mesopotamia. We have seen that the Sufyanid caliphs formed strong ties with the Quda'a. When Umayyad authority tottered after the death of Yazid, Qays came out in support of Ibn al-Zubayr while Quda'a eventually decided to give their support to Marwan. The two confederations met in battle at Marj Rahit near Damascus in the summer of 684, and it was the victory of Quda'a and its allies at this battle which ensured the continuation of Umayyad rule, at least in southern and central Syria. The remaining years of the civil war, though, were marked by a long and complicated period of tribal feuding in the Syrian desert and in Mesopotamia, a bitter legacy of the battle of Marj Rahit. It was in the course of these feuds that the distinction between 'northerners' and 'southerners' became more clearly established. Quda'a, who had been regarded previously as descendants of Isma'il, that is 'northerners', now came to regard themselves as 'southerners' like their allies and in contradistinction to the 'northern' Qays. This provided the nomenclature for the factionalism in Syria for the remainder of the Umayyad period: on the one side Kalb, the dominant tribe of the 'southern' Quda'a; on the other Qays, the leaders of the 'northerners'.[11]

In Basra, the factions appear under different names. There the original settlers consisted mainly of two tribal groups both classed as 'northerners': Mudar, under the leadership of the tribe of Tamim, and Rabi'a. Shortly before the second civil war a third group, the 'southern' Azd from Oman, migrated into Basra in large numbers, and an alliance was made between them and Rabi'a against the Mudar. After the death of Yazid, the Umayyad governor of Iraq, 'Ubayd Allah b. Ziyad, tried to get himself recognised in Basra as *amir* by the Arabs there until affairs regarding the caliphate were cleared up. The Mudar, led by Tamim, refused to accept him and a feud then developed between the Mudar on one side and Azd and Rabi'a on the other. Eventually this feud was temporarily settled and Basra came under Zubayrid control. But the parties had been formed for future conflict, and what is particularly important is that it was from Basra that Khurasan was garrisoned and so the divisions of Basra were carried over to this key province of the north-east frontier. In the east, therefore, the factions generally go under the names of Mudar, the 'northerners', including Tamim and Qays, and Yemen, the 'southerners', dominated by Azd but including also the formally 'northern' Rabi'a tribes.[12]

The underlying factors leading to the polarisation of the tribesmen in this way have already been discussed. In both Syria and Basra we can point to two things in particular which probably had a crucial influence. First, in the period before the second civil war, the existing tribal balance or situation had been upset in both places by recent immigration. In northern Syria and Mesopotamia there had been recent migrations of Qays, while in Basra the recent arrival of Azd gave Rabi'a the opportunity to attack the domination of Tamim. Secondly, in both places the political situation became entangled with the tribal one. In Syria the Sufyanid links with Quda'a may have provoked Qaysi support for Ibn al-Zubayr, while in Basra 'Ubayd Allah b. Ziyad's attempt to get Azd to support his bid to be recognised as *amir* in the face of Tamim's hostility seems to have triggered off the fighting. The dangers resulting from the government's reliance on or support for one faction at the expense of another are self-evident.

In looking at the second civil war generally, and seeking to assess its significance and consequences, therefore, it seems that the conflict between the Umayyads and Ibn al-Zubayr, although it supplies the thread which provides the distinctive colour of this *fitna*, is not its most important element. Ibn al-Zubayr left behind no party or programme, and if he had been victorious it is not clear what changes would have resulted apart from the end of Umayyad rule and its replacement by that of another member of Quraysh.[13] To some extent this judgement may need to be qualified by reference to the development of the Muslim sanctuary. It might be possible to argue that the struggle with Ibn al-Zubayr was decisive in establishing that the Muslim sanctuary would be at Mecca, away from the seat of the caliph, but this is a complicated issue which involves questioning the Muslim tradition's insistence that the sanctuary had been fixed at Mecca since the time of the Prophet. The most obvious result of this second civil war is, of course, the change from Sufyanid to Marwanid rule, but the more significant consequences are elsewhere. First, the polarisation of the Arab factions provides the basis for divisions among the Arabs which, as we will see, were of the greatest importance for the Umayyad state. Secondly, the impetus given to the development of Shi'ism and the link between this and the later anti-Umayyad movement of the Hashimiyya have been indicated. Next, the emergence of the *mawali* as a significant force for the first time is also a pointer for future developments. Another development, of a somewhat more temporary importance, but for a time a major problem for the Umayyads, was the appearance of Kharijite groups in Iraq and Mesopotamia, taking advantage of the breakdown of order there during the troubles associated with Mukhtar and the Zubayrid rule. After the reassertion of Umayyad authority in the area, 'Abd al-Malik's governor, al-Hajjaj, had to devote considerable time and effort to the threat they posed. Finally, the second civil war had revealed the shaky foundations of the Sufyanid system of government, especially in Iraq where the *ashraf* had given their support to the Zubayrids. The questionable loyalty of the Iraqis in general and particularly the *ashraf* was to be revealed in episodes after the end of the civil war, and was probably decisive in the development of a more direct type of rule by 'Abd al-Malik and his descendants.

Notes

1. The most recent detailed discussion with full bibliography is Gernot Rotter, *Die Umayyaden und der zweite Bürgerkrieg (680–692)*. See also R. Sellheim, *Der zweite Bürgerkrieg im Islam*. In English, A. A. Dixon, *The Umayyad caliphate 65–86/684–705*, treats in detail some of the later episodes.
2. J. Wellhausen, *Arab kingdom*, 140–5; H. Lammens, *Le califat de Yazid 1er*, 98–106; Gernot Rotter, *Bürgerkrieg*, 35–6.
3. J. Wellhausen, *Arab kingdom*, 167–9; F. Buhl, 'Die Krisis der Umajjadenherrschaft im Jahre 684', *ZA*, 27 (1912); H. Lammens, 'Mo'awia II ou le dernier des Sofianides', in *Le siècle des Omayyades*, 163–210.
4. J. Wellhausen, *Arab kingdom*, 147–65; article 'al-Harra' in *EI2*; M. J. Kister, 'The battle of the Harra', in *Studies in memory of Gaston Wiet*, ed. M. Rosen Ayalon, Jerusalem, 1977; H. Lammens, *Yazid 1er*, 210–57; G. Rotter, *Bürgerkrieg*, 40–53.
5. J. Wellhausen, *Arab kingdom*, 165–7; H. Lammens, *Yazid 1er*, 257–69; G. Rotter, *Bürgerkrieg*, 53–59.
6. J. Wellhausen, *Arab kingdom*, 170–200; A. A. Dixon, *Umayyad caliphate*, 121–42; G. Rotter, *Bürgerkrieg*, 107 ff.; article "Abd Allah ibn al-Zubayr' in *EI2*.
7. Article 'Ka'ba' in *EI2*; J. Wellhausen, *Arab Kingdom*, 212–15; S. D. Goitein, 'The historical background of the erection of the Dome of the Rock', *JAOS*, 70 (1950). See further below, pp. 59–61.
8. J. Wellhausen, *Religio-political factions*, 105–20; H. Lammens, *Yazid 1er*, 117–81; articles 'al-Husayn b. 'Ali' and 'Karbala' in *EI2*; S. M. Jafri, *Origins and early development of Shi'a Islam*, 174 ff.; G. Rotter, *Bürgerkrieg*, 37–40.
9. G. E. von Grunebaum, *Muslim festivals*, 85–94.
10. J. Wellhausen, *Religio-political factions*, 121–59; articles 'Al-Mukhtar' and 'Muhammad b. al-Hanafiyya' in *EI1*, 'Kaysaniyya' in *EI2*; K. A. Fariq, 'The story of an Arab diplomat', *Studies in Islam*, 3 (1966) and 4 (1967); W. M. Watt, 'Shi'ism under the Umayyads', *JRAS* (1960); A. A. Dixon, *Umayyad caliphate*, 25–81; S. M. Jafri, *Origins and early development of Shi'a Islam*, 235 ff.; M. A. Shaban, *New interpretation*, 94–6; G. Rotter, *Bürgerkrieg*, 93–106, 187–92.

11. J. Wellhausen, *Arab kingdom*, 170–83, 201–9; A. A. Dixon, *Umayyad caliphate*, 83–120; P. Crone, *Slaves on horses*, 34–6; G. Rotter, *Bürgerkrieg*, 126–51.
12. J. Wellhausen, *Arab kingdom*, 209–10, 397–411; G. Rotter, *Bürgerkrieg*, 68–84. See genealogical tables 1 and 2, above.
13. G. Rotter, *Bürgerkrieg*, 243–51.

Chapter 5

'Abd al-Malik and al-Hajjaj

After Marwan's accession to the caliphate in 684 all of the remainder of the Umayyad caliphs were descended directly from him. It is remarkable that his son 'Abd al-Malik (caliph 685–705) was himself succeeded in the caliphate by no fewer than four of his own sons, the succession of the brothers continuing down until 743 and being interrupted only by the brief caliphate of their cousin 'Umar b. 'Abd al-'Aziz (717–20).[1] 'Abd al-Malik's immediate successor was his eldest son al-Walid I (705–15) and his rule seems hardly differentiated from that of his father, for, almost from the time when the civil war ended until shortly before the death of al-Walid, the dominant figure in the sources is the governor of Iraq and viceroy of the east al-Hajjaj (governor 694–714). Like his predecessor Ziyad, we tend to hear more about him than about the caliphs in Syria and he thus serves to give a unity to the period of 'Abd al-Malik and al-Walid. This period, although not without its problems for the government, was in some ways the high point of Umayyad power, witnessing significant territorial advances both in the east and the west and the emergence of a more marked Arabic and Islamic character in the state's public face. Before discussing the period following the civil war, however, there are some developments in the earlier part of 'Abd al-Malik's caliphate which need to be noted.

First, the grip of the Marwanids on the caliphate was tightened. At the meeting which discussed the future of the caliphate before Marj Rahit in 684 the Marwanids had not been the only branch of the Umayyad family in contention, and acceptance of Marwan seems to have been secured only at the price of guarantees regarding the future right of succession of some of the other contenders. The claims of the surviving members of the family of Yazid b. Mu'awiya may have been sidestepped by Marwan's marriage to Yazid's widow Fakhita. Indeed some sources say that Marwan's refusal to honour the promises he had made about the succession of

58

Khalid the son of Yazid led Fakhita to poison her new husband. A stronger rival of Marwan was 'Amr b. Sa'id al-Ashdaq of another branch of the Umayyad family, whose seniority was indicated by the fact that he had been governor of Medina for a while under Yazid. When 'Abd al-Malik succeeded Marwan, 'Amr felt that the guarantees made before Marj Rahit had not been honoured, and, in 689–90, taking advantage of the absence of 'Abd al-Malik in the field against the Zubayrids, he revolted and seized Damascus. 'Abd al-Malik had to abandon his expedition and on his return to Damascus he had 'Amr b. Sa'id killed, apparently after promising him a safe conduct.[2]

Marwan had planned it that he should be succeeded by his two sons, 'Abd al-Malik and 'Abd al-'Aziz, one after the other, and had had the oath of allegiance taken for them while he still ruled. When 'Abd al-Malik became caliph his brother 'Abd al-'Aziz was appointed to be his governor of Egypt. There then arose a tension, which became quite common in the Marwanid period, between the ruler's desire to pass on the caliphate to his own children and the previous caliph's arrangement of the succession. 'Abd al-Malik tried without success to get 'Abd al-'Aziz to give up his claims to the caliphate, and it was only the death of the latter shortly before that of the caliph which prevented a possible dispute over this question. In view of the potentiality for conflict inherent in the lack of a fixed order of succession to the caliphate in the Umayyad period, it is remarkable how seldom real trouble developed from it. When it did, as in the third civil war following the death of Hisham in 743, it was because the succession issue was bound up with others.

Apart from the difficulties caused by the feuds between Kalb and Qays after the battle of Marj Rahit, which continued in Syria and Mesopotamia even after the ending of the second civil war, the other important and interesting occurrence involving 'Abd al-Malik in the early part of his caliphate was his building of the Dome of the Rock in Jerusalem. The original inscription which he had put inside the Dome tells us that it was built by 'Abd al-Malik in the year 72 (that is, AD 692). In spite of a recent attempt to argue that this date refers to the beginning of the building, it is more likely, and is generally accepted, that it is the date of its completion. In other words, the conception and construction of the Dome occurred while the second civil war was still in progress, while Arabia and Iraq were still in the hands of the Zubayrids. K. A. C. Cresswell suggested a date between 684 and 687 for the beginning of the building.

The Dome of the Rock has been the subject of considerable speculation and controversy. We have no clear and uncontestable statement about why 'Abd al-Malik built it, what function the building was intended to have (it is not, for example, a mosque), the significance of the site which it occupies (it may be questioned whether the traditional association between the rock over which it is built and the miraculous ascension of Muhammad to heaven, the *mi'raj*, existed at the time when it was built), or its relationship to other Muslim sacred places and buildings. Attention has centred especially on this last question. Some of the Muslim sources say that it was built to provide a focus for a pilgrimage to Jerusalem which would rival the Ka'ba at Mecca, at that time under Ibn al-Zubayr's control. While some modern scholars have accepted this view, and sought to relate the Dome to what they saw as a more general Umayyad policy to build up the religious significance of Jerusalem at the expense of the holy places in the Hijaz, others have argued that it relies too much on the tendentious anti-Umayyad outlook of the Muslim tradition. If the Dome was meant or used as a centre of pilgrimage, the latter argue, this could only have been intended as a temporary measure, since no Muslim ruler could risk being regarded as an enemy of the pilgrimage to Mecca (the *hajj*), one of the five 'pillars of Islam' and a fundamental duty which had been imposed in the time of the Prophet. Those who adopt this latter position tend to see the Dome as an expression of cultural and religious assertiveness on the part of 'Abd al-Malik directed particularly at the Christians, the previously dominant religious group in Syria. Some support for this interpretation can be gathered from passages in some sources and from the inscriptions of the Dome itself.[3]

Nevertheless, to interpret the Dome as primarily an expression of Muslim self-confidence, or as an attempt to outshine the Christian religious buildings of Jerusalem and Syria, possibly underestimates the significance of the site on which it was built and isolates it from other developments involving the sanctuary in the second civil war. Whatever specifically Muslim associations came to be attached to the rock over which the Dome was built, at the time it was generally held, by Muslims, Jews and Christians, to be part of the ancient Jewish Temple of Jerusalem. As such it had great cosmological significance and was regarded as the centre of the world, although Christians had transferred several of the cosmological notions to Christian holy places such as the church of the Holy Sepulchre and

Mount Calvary. This alone makes it likely that the Dome of the Rock was to have a unique importance. In addition, Jewish apocalyptic ideas expected the coming of a king who would restore the Temple (destroyed by the Romans in AD 70), and it seems likely that 'Abd al-Malik's uniquely magnificent edifice would be put in this context. Finally, it has already been noted that Ibn al-Zubayr seems to have identified himself with the Ka'ba at Mecca and that the second civil war saw the repeated demolition and rebuilding of Ibn al-Zubayr's sanctuary. It seems logical, therefore, to see the building of the Dome of the Rock against the background of arguments about the sanctuary in the second civil war and to see it as a contender for the role of the Muslim sanctuary. That it did not achieve this status, and that when Mecca came under Umayyad control its Ka'ba was accepted as the sanctuary by all Muslims, need not reflect on 'Abd al-Malik's intentions when he built it.

Whatever the significance of the Dome of the Rock at the time when it was built, it stands out as one of the earliest surviving concrete expressions of the new religion and civilisation of Islam which was beginning to emerge in the lands which had been conquered by the Arabs. Apart from its innovative architecture (which is not to say, of course, that it is unrelated to previous architecture), two things in particular are noteworthy. First, the inscriptions in the Dome contained passages which may be recognised, in spite of one or two minor variants from the Koran as we know it, as Koranic. These are the earliest securely datable examples of Koranic texts to have survived. Secondly, the texts refer to Islam as 'the religion of truth', and this is the first certain evidence of Islam as the name of the religion of the Arabs; earlier non-Muslim literary texts do not call the Arabs Muslim or refer to their religion as Islam.[4]

Changes in Government and Administration

The early Marwanid period saw a gradual move away from the indirect system of rule of the Sufyanids to a more centralised and direct form of government. The middlemen, the *ashraf* and the various non-Arab notables, who had stood between the government and the subjects, were replaced by officials more directly responsible to the caliph and his governors. The stimulus for this, no doubt, was provided by the second civil war when loyalty

to the Umayyads had proved so fragile, and the weaknesses thus
revealed were underlined by subsequent events, especially the
revolt of Ibn al-Ash'ath (see below) in the early eighth century,
when the hostility of the *ashraf* was against manifested. Furthermore, numbers of non-Arabs now began to accept Islam and
become *mawali* while many Arabs ceased to have a primarily
military role and turned to occupations like trade. The gradual
breakdown of the barriers between the Arabs and the subject
peoples which ensued meant that the old system, which depended
upon isolation of the conquerors from the conquered peoples,
became less feasible.[5]

One of the important changes which came about in response to
these political and social developments was the formation of
something like a standing army at the service of the government, in
place of the reliance on the mass of Arab tribesmen which had been
characteristic of the Sufyanids. In the Marwanid period we hear, for
the first time, of Syrian troops being sent to the provinces to keep
order and to participate in campaigns, while it is clear that in the
provinces only some of the Arabs joined the army, others adopting
a more civilian way of life. At the same time the governors
appointed tended to be military men, having risen in the army,
unlike those of the Sufyanids who depended on their tribal standing
or relationship to the caliph. Symptomatic of the change is that we
now no longer hear of the meetings between the *ashraf* and the
governor in the latter's *majlis* or of the delegations (*wufud*) of local
notables to the caliph's court in Syria, both characteristic of the time
of Mu'awiya and Yazid.

To some extent this development is obscured by the fact that the
sources continue to use Arab tribal terminology when referring to
the army: such terms as *qa'id* for a commander or *qawm* and *qabila*
for the men were originally tribal terms, and the rival factions which
emerged in the provinces during the Marwanid period bear the
names of the tribal confederations, Mudar and Yemen. Yet this is
rather misleading. What we have are not tribes in arms as in the old
days, but factions in an army, made up of men of tribal origin
certainly (and factional alignment usually, but not invariably,
coincides with tribal origin), but not tribes in the real sense. Arabs
not enrolled in the army were not involved in the factions, but non-
Arabs in the army were. The development of these factions does not
become evident until after the death of al-Hajjaj, but such things as
the use of the Syrians as a sort of imperial army and the tendency to

rely on military men as governors do begin in his time. Indeed al-Hajjaj himself, although a Thaqafi, is an example of an individual who rose to power from comparatively humble origins through service in the army.[6]

Certain innovations in the system of administration and bureaucracy which are associated with 'Abd al-Malik also strengthen the impression of a trend to a greater centralisation of government. In the classical Muslim state as it developed in the 'Abbasid period, a government department or ministry is called a *diwan*. The origins of both the word and the institution are rather obscure. Tradition tells us that the first *diwan* was instituted by the caliph 'Umar I (634-44) and that at that time the word referred to the register of soldiers and pensions due to them which 'Umar had compiled. However, the word seems to have taken on its meaning of 'government department' already by the time of the first Umayyad, Mu'awiya, who is said to have had a *diwan* for the collection of taxes and to have introduced two for the government chancery — one for the writing of documents and one for the sealing of documents (the *dīwān al-rasā'il* and the *dīwān al-khātam*). However, the main business of the administration remained the assessment and collection of taxes, and in a general sense the *diwan* refers to the administration. 'Abd al-Malik is generally credited with changing the official language of the *diwan* to Arabic.

After the Arab conquest of the Middle East, as is to be expected, the previously existing administrative systems in the various provinces were left as far as possible intact: not only did officials who had served the Byzantines and Sasanids continue to serve the Arabs, the administration continued to use the languages which had been in use before the conquest, Greek, Coptic and Persian (Pahlevi). The change to Arabic as the sole official administrative language, the arabisation of the *diwan*, is generally associated with 'Abd al-Malik and al-Hajjaj although there is some obscurity about dates and circumstances. Some sources, for instance, attribute the measure to al-Walid I rather than to his father, and the report which says that the change of language was introduced in response to the boorish behaviour of a Greek clerk who had urinated in an inkwell should be seen as an example of the anecdotal explanation of major gradual changes which mediaeval sources delight in. At any rate the evidence of the papyri does bear out the claim that Arabic began to be the official language of administration from about the beginning of the eighth century AD although the change was not made overnight and it was not until almost the end of the Umayyad period that Arabic became the language of administration in border provinces like Khurasan. What effect the change had or was intended to have on the ethnic origin of the personnel of the administration is difficult to say. It seems that the bureaucrats continued to be overwhelmingly of non-Arab descent, that is *mawali*, although as time passed the distinction between Arab and non-Arab became increasingly less clear-cut. Equally, it is possible that the move to Arabic was intended to encourage the acquisition of the language by the subject peoples but, on the other hand, the very fact that the changeover could begin necessarily indicates that already by this time there must have been a considerable number of potential bureaucrats with at least sufficient Arabic for the requirements of the administration.[7]

One of the *diwans* of the mediaeval Islamic administration occupied itself with the running of the *barid*. The *barid* was a sort of communications system, consisting of routes linking the main centres of the empire along which there were stations with horses at the ready so that messengers could come and go quickly between the provinces and the metropolis. Although theoretically a postal system, in effect it was an instrument for keeping the government informed about developments in the provinces, and the provincial controllers of the *barid* were local spies on behalf of the central government. Here again Muslim tradition gives to 'Abd al-Malik an important role in the organisation of the *barid* system, although the possibly Greek or Latin etymology of the word suggests the continuation of a former Byzantine institution, and one often feels that Muslim tradition finds figures like 'Umar and 'Abd al-Malik convenient personalities with which to associate institutions or developments which it considers must have a decisive beginning but about which precise details are lacking.[8]

Another important development, again focusing on 'Abd al-Malik and al-Hajjaj, is the introduction, for the first time, of a specifically Muslim coinage. As with the languages of administration, so with the coinage: the Arab conquerors had taken over and only slightly adapted the Byzantine and Sasanid coins which were in circulation, and the mints which had produced these coins continued to do so for the Arabs. The minting of gold coins was a Byzantine imperial prerogative, and the Arabs continued to import gold coins from Byzantium. In this way the pre-conquest gold denarius, silver drachma and copper follis became the Arab *dinar*, *dirham* and *fils*. Some experiments with a new type of coinage made by the Sufyanid rulers proved unsuccessful, and it was not until the 690s, both in Syria and in Iraq, that 'Abd al-Malik and al-Hajjaj began to mint coins of a decisively new type, allegedly in response to a threat by the Byzantine ruler to stamp the gold coins exported to the Arabs with anti-Muslim formulae.

The most important characteristic of the new coinage was the fact that it was purely epigraphic. The faces of the coins were inscribed only with Muslim religious formulae, not with the portraits of rulers or other pictorial representations which had marked the Byzantine and Sasanid as well as some of the earlier Arab coins. This was a decisive break with numismatic tradition, and provided the model which Muslim coins have generally, but not always, followed since.[9]

The lack of pictorial imagery is also a striking characteristic of the Dome of the Rock and other early Islamic religious and public buildings. Opposition to the figural representation of human beings and animals is a marked feature of the Muslim religious tradition (as it is in Judaism), but this has not prevented a flourishing tradition of representational art at a popular or private level where the influence of the religious scholars was more remote. There are vigorous and even beautiful representations of human beings and animals, for example, in the lodges and palaces which the Umayyads built for themselves outside the towns. How far opposition to this sort of pictorial representation was a feature of early Islam, and the sources of Muslim hostility to such sculpture and painting, are questions which have received considerable discussion. There is some evidence to indicate that the iconoclastic movement in Byzantium, which came to the fore under Leo III (717–41), was in part a response to developments in the Muslim world, and the caliph Yazid II (720–4) is known to have undertaken attacks on the images and statues of his Christian subjects in Syria. (For further details, see O. Grabar, *The formation of Islamic art*, 75–103; P. Crone, 'Islam, Judeo-Christianity, and Byzantine iconoclasm'; and G. R. D. King, 'Islam, iconoclasm and the declaration of doctrine', *BSOAS*, 48 (1985).)

Taken together, the innovations of the early Marwanid period in the field of administration and coinage help to strengthen the impression of an administration becoming more centralised and uniform. Furthermore, they add to the evidence provided by the new monumental buildings — not only the Dome of the Rock but also the mosque of the Prophet in Medina and the mosque in

Damascus which incorporated the former church of St John, both built by al-Walid[10] — of the emergence of a new and distinctive Arab Muslim state and culture from what had begun as, in some ways, a Byzantine or Sasanid successor state.

Al-Hajjaj in Iraq

Al-Hajjaj b. Yusuf al-Thaqafi, governor of Iraq and the east under 'Abd al-Malik and al-Walid from 694 to 714, is presented as the instrument, and to some extent as the instigator, of these administrative changes. Having come to prominence in the campaigns against the Zubayrids, when he had commanded the final attack on Ibn al-Zubayr, he was for a time governor of the Hijaz for 'Abd al-Malik before being sent to Iraq. His arrival in Kufa in 694 is marked in the sources by a famous introductory *khutba* in the mosque, often cited as an example of Arab eloquence and reminiscent of the *khutba* attributed to his Thaqafi predecessor in Iraq, Ziyad: 'I see heads which have become ripe and ready for plucking, and I behold blood between the turbans and the beards.'[11]

Al-Hajjaj's immediate problem in Iraq was a threat from the Kharijites, a legacy of the breakdown of order there in the second civil war, which was made worse by the reluctance of the Iraqi soldiers to undertake campaigns against them. The threat came from two directions. In the south and east, threatening Basra, the group known as the Azariqa had been a danger even during the Zubayrid rule in Iraq. Al-Muhallab b. Abi Sufra had been entrusted with suppressing the movement by Mus'ab b. al-Zubayr, and when Iraq submitted to the Umayyads he transferred his allegiance too. When al-Hajjaj arrived in Iraq, al-Muhallab was in the field against the Azariqa but was having difficulty in holding his army together. Shortly after al-Hajjaj's arrival, a second Kharijite outbreak occurred, this time to the north, and a source of danger to Kufa. The leader of this second rising was Shabib b. Yazid.

Al-Hajjaj's harsh policy against those who would not join al-Muhallab achieved its purpose and the Azariqa were gradually pushed out of Iraq into the neighbouring Persian provinces and then further east into the province of Sistan so that by the end of the seventh century they were no longer a danger for the central authority. The danger from Shabib was also overcome when, in 697, he and his followers were defeated and Shabib himself drowned while attempting to flee over the river Dujayl in Ahwaz.[12] Victory over Shabib had only been achieved, though, after troops had been brought from Syria to Iraq. This was an important new development soon to be followed elsewhere. It seems that the troops were not sent back when the Kharijite menace was over but, indeed, were soon reinforced by further Syrian detachments. Apparently a new way of supporting the authority of the Umayyad governor over the troublesome Iraqi garrison towns had been introduced.

The transfer of the Syrian forces to Iraq made necessary the provision of quarters for them, and it was this need which led to the construction of a new garrison town in Iraq in the early years of the eighth century. This was the town of Wasit, so called, apparently, because of its 'middle' position between Kufa, Basra and the old Sasanid capital at Ctesiphon (al-Mada'in). Wasit now became the Syrian garrison town in Iraq, but, whatever the intentions at the time of its foundation, it did not displace Kufa and Basra in importance in other respects and it did not become the regular residence of the Umayyad governors.[13]

As well as bringing in the Syrians, al-Hajjaj had decreased the pay of the Iraqi soldiers which, we are told, the Zubayrids had raised in an attempt to secure their loyalty against the Umayyads. This does not seem to have endeared him to them, and it increased their unwillingness to participate in campaigns at his command. Right from the beginning, therefore, al-Hajjaj was faced with a number of rebellions on the part of the Iraqi soldiers, sometimes even allegedly in league with the Kharijites. Most of these rebellions were suppressed without undue difficulty,[14] but one of them, in the early years of the eighth century, came close to destroying al-Hajjaj's power in Iraq. This was the revolt led by 'Abd al-Rahman b. al-Ash'ath, which is generally dated from about 700 to 703 although there is some doubt about the precise chronology.[15]

Ibn al-Ash'ath was a descendant of the leading family of the 'southern' tribe of Kinda. His grandfather, after resisting the early Muslims in the Ridda wars which followed the death of Muhammad, had participated in the conquests and settled in Kufa. He and his sons were leading members of the *ashraf* of that town and played a prominent part in its affairs. About 700, al-Hajjaj appointed Ibn al-Ash'ath to the command of an army to be sent to Sistan where an earlier force had been badly defeated by the still independent ruler of the kingdom of Zabulistan, roughly modern Afghanistan, known in the sources as Zunbil. The army sent under

Ibn al-Ash'ath's command is known in tradition as the 'army of peacocks', usually interpreted as a reference to their splendid equipment but sometimes as an allusion to the proud and haughty manner of the Kufan soldiers and *ashraf* who composed it.

In Sistan the army mutinied. It is reported that al-Hajjaj had ordered an immediate attack against Zunbil, but Ibn al-Ash'ath wanted more time to prepare and had the support of his army in this. The immediate cause of the mutiny, it is said, was the tone of a letter from al-Hajjaj ordering an immediate advance. What seems clear is that the soldiers were unhappy at the prospect of a long and difficult campaign so far from Iraq. Allegiance was therefore given to Ibn al-Ash'ath and the decision taken to march back to Iraq to drive out al-Hajjaj.

On the march back the army was joined by Iraqi malcontents from the other garrisons they passed on the way, and by the time the army reached Fars the decision had been made to reject the caliph 'Abd al-Malik as well as al-Hajjaj. Although the revolt was sparked off by specific military grievances, it was inevitable, given the interaction of religion and politics in early Muslim society, that it should take on a religious flavour. Highly coloured religious language is attributed to both sides, the rebels referring to al-Hajjaj as the enemy of God and comparing him to Pharaoh.

Meanwhile al-Hajjaj had received reinforcements in the shape of a further influx of troops from Syria, and he marched out to meet the rebels on the river Dujayl. This battle, however, ended in a victory for Ibn al-Ash'ath and his men, and al-Hajjaj's fleeing army was pursued to Basra where it managed to gain control of one of the suburbs and score a limited victory over the rebels.

The principal focus of the revolt, though, was Kufa, the base of Ibn al-Ash'ath and the *ashraf*. The main part of the rebel army left Basra for Kufa, leaving only a small force behind and thus enabling al-Hajjaj to get control of most of Basra. He then pursued the rebels to Kufa, camping on the right bank of the Euphrates at some distance from the town in order to secure his communications with Syria. By this time the revolt had won the support of most of the men of religion known in the sources as the *qurra'* (usually understood as Koran 'readers') and had acquired a significant religious hue.[16] 'Abd al-Malik appears to have tried to hedge his bets by negotiating with the rebels and even, reportedly, offering to remove al-Hajjaj from office, while at the same time sending reinforcements to his Iraqi governor. But the rebels appear to have been so confident that they felt no need to compromise.

The decisive battle, or rather prolonged period of skirmishing, took place at a site called Dayr al-Jamajim, which has not been securely identified. It occupied the late spring and early summer although there is some doubt about the year. Eventually, the rebel force began to disintegrate, encouraged by offers of pardon from al-Hajjaj for those who would submit. Again, as in previous rebellions and civil wars, a contrast appears between the discipline and organisation of the Umayyads and their largely Syrian support and the lack of these qualities among their opponents in spite of, or perhaps rather because of, the more righteous and religious flavour of the opposition. Eventually, al-Hajjaj was able to enter Kufa where he pardoned those who would submit, providing they would admit that in revolting they had renounced Islam, while he executed those who would not make this admission.

The remnants of Ibn al-Ash'ath's army fled first to Basra then to Khuzistan in southwest Persia, where the Syrians pursued and defeated them thanks to a surprise night attack through the marshes. The survivors, including Ibn al-Ash'ath, now fled east back to Sistan, and the revolt was mopped up. When the Umayyad pursuers arrived in Sistan, many of the rebels tried to flee north to Herat but were rounded up by the governor of Khurasan, Yazid b. al-Muhallab, son of al-Hajjaj's general who had defeated the Kharijites in Iraq. Yazid, however, treated the Yemenis among the rebels fairly leniently and only sent the Mudaris to al-Hajjaj in Wasit. The fate of Ibn al-Ash'ath himself is somewhat obscure. We are told that he took refuge with Zunbil, but the latter was persuaded by al-Hajjaj's representative to surrender him. Some say he committed suicide in order to prevent this, others that Zunbil killed him and handed his head over to the Umayyad authority in Sistan.[17]

Ibn al-Ash'ath's revolt was fundamentally a revolt of the Iraqi soldiery and especially the *ashraf* against what they perceived as an Umayyad attempt to supplant them. It was not, as some nineteenth-century scholars argued, brought about by the *mawali* and their grievances against the Umayyad government, although it is clear that the *mawali* supported it. Neither was it an expression of the factionalism which was to become so important later. The fact that Ibn al-Ash'ath and most of his supporters were Yemenis merely reflects the fact that the Yemenis were the dominant tribal element in Kufa, and, although al-Hajjaj as a Thaqafi was genealogically a 'northerner', the commander of his Syrian troops was a 'southerner' of Kalb. Regarding the religious polemic used by both sides, most of it is stereotyped, unspecific and to be found in other contexts. The accusation made by the rebels that the government had caused the death of the ritual prayer (*imātat al-ṣalāt*), and the battle cry of the *qurra'* at Dayr al-Jamajim, 'revenge for the ritual prayer' (*yā tharāt al-ṣalāt*), however, seem more specific and may indicate that conduct of the ritual prayer was one of the issues between the government and the religious supporters of Ibn al-Ash'ath.

Although not primarily a movement of the *mawali*, the participation in the revolt by the *mawali* and the *qurra'* indicates that it was not only the Iraqi soldiery who had grievances against the government, and it was the combination of forces against al-Hajjaj which made the revolt so dangerous. The participation of the *mawali*, many of whom were included among the *qurra'*, is associated with a phenomenon which first becomes important during the time of al-Hajjaj's governorship in Iraq — the influx into the garrison towns of large numbers of former non-Arab cultivators who now abandon their lands and attempt to enter Islam by becoming the clients (*mawali*) of Arabs in the garrison towns. These *mawali* are to be distinguished from the prisoners of war and others who had earlier been prominent among the supporters of Mukhtar. Among their motives in leaving their fields and villages at this particular time, the desire to escape taxation and the hope of finding a new livelihood in the towns, most likely by enrolment in the army, were undoubtedly to the forefront. A similar phenomenon is attested in Egypt, where, however, the peasants sought to avoid taxation by leaving their own tax districts and fleeing to another or into a monastery (monks initially having exemption from taxation). It seems that the early Marwanid period, with its increased centralisation, saw a greater efficiency in tax collection and that the cultivators regarded flight from their lands as the only means of escape. The question of the nature of the taxes involved will be taken up later.

Al-Hajjaj, faced with a decline in the revenue from taxation, reacted by rounding up the *mawali* in the towns, driving them out and forcing them to pay their taxes, stamping their hands as a token of the tax having been paid (in Egypt 'passports' have been found which indicate that the bearer has paid his taxes). The result was the hostility not only of the *mawali* who were treated in this way, but also of the religious opponents of the Umayyads who saw the policy as an attack on the principle of an Islam open to all and conferring equality of rights. This was the first sign of the conflict between the demands of Islam and the need of the government for revenue which was to become increasingly important for the Umayyads.[18]

Notes

1. See Genealogical Table 3.

2. J. Wellhausen, *Arab kingdom*, 183, 188–90; A. A. Dixon, *Umayyad caliphate*, 124–28; G. Rotter, *Bürgerkrieg*, 166–9; article "Amir b. Sa'id al-Ashdak' in *EI2*.

3. I. Goldziher, *Muslim Studies*, ii, 44 ff.; K. A. C. Cresswell, *A short account of early Muslim architecture*, 17 ff.; S. D. Goitein, 'The sanctity of Jerusalem and Palestine in early Islam' in his *Studies in Islamic history and institutions*; O. Grabar, 'The Umayyad Dome of the Rock in Jerusalem', *Ars Orientalis*, 3 (1959); for the argument that the inscription date refers to the beginning of the building, see G. Rotter, *Bürgerkrieg*, 227–30.

4. M. A. Cook and P. Crone, *Hagarism*, 18 and note 25; C. Kessler, "Abd al-Malik's inscription in the Dome of the Rock: a reconsideration', *JRAS*, (1970).

5. P. Crone, *Slaves on horses*, 37–41, 49–57.

6. J. Wellhausen, *Arab kingdom*, 371–3; P. Crone, *Slaves on horses*, 37–40.

7. Article 'Diwan' in *EI2*; M. Sprengling, 'Persian into Arabic', *AJSL* (1939 and 1940).

8. Article 'Barid' in *EI2*; for the late Roman *cursus publicus*, in which system the saddle horses used for the express post were called *veredi*, see A. H. M. Jones, *The later Roman Empire, 284–602*, 830–34. See also F. Dvornik, *Origins of intelligence services* (I owe this reference to Dr D. O. Morgan).

9. J. Walker, *A catalogue of the Arab-Byzantine and the post-reform Umaiyad coins*; P. Grierson, 'The monetary reforms of 'Abd al-Malik', *JESHO*, 3 (1960).

10. K. A. C. Cresswell, *A short account of early Muslim architecture*, 43 ff.; J. Sauvaget, *La mosquée omeyyade de Medine*.

11. Article 'al-Hadjdjadj b. Yusuf' in *EI2*.

12. J. Wellhausen, *Religio-political factions*, 61–83; A. A. Dixon, *Umayyad caliphate*, 169–98.

13. Article 'Wasit' in *EI1*; K. A. C. Cresswell, *A short account of early Muslim architecture*, 40–2; O. Grabar, 'Al-Mushatta, Baghdad and Wasit', in J. Kritzeck and R. Bayly Winder (ed.), *The world of Islam. Studies in honour of Philip K. Hitti*, London, 1959, especially 103 ff.

14. J. Wellhausen, *Arab kingdom*, 228–31; A. A. Dixon, *Umayyad caliphate*, 143–51.

15. For a detailed discussion with extensive references to sources, see Redwan Sayed, *Die Revolte des Ibn al-As'at und die Koranleser*.

16. For an attempted redefinition of the *qurra'*, see M. A. Shaban, *New interpretation*, 23; G. H. A. Juynboll, 'The qurra' in early Islamic history', *JESHO*, 16 (1973), and his subsequent articles on the same theme in *JSS*, 19 (1974) and *ZDMG*, 125 (1975).

17. J. Wellhausen, *Arab kingdom*, 254 ff.; A. A. Dixon, *Umayyad caliphate*, 151–68; M. A. Shaban, *New interpretation*, 110–11; article 'Ibn al-Ash'ath' in *EI2*; for the background to the sending of Ibn al-Ash'ath to Sistan, see C. E. Bosworth, "Ubaidallah b. Abi Bakra and the "army of destruction" in Zabulistan', *Isl.*, 50 (1973).

18. J. Wellhausen, *Arab kingdom*, 279–80, 285–6.

Chapter 6

The Development of Factionalism and the Problems of Islamisation

The death of al-Walid in 715 was followed by three relatively short caliphates. His brother Sulayman ruled for two years (715–17) and he in turn was then succeeded by his cousin 'Umar b. 'Abd al-'Aziz, 'Umar II, from 717 until 720. Another son of 'Abd al-Malik, Yazid II, succeeded 'Umar II from 720 until 724. The last of the sons of 'Abd al-Malik to become caliph was Hisham (723–43). These sons of 'Abd al-Malik were appointed in what was becoming the usual way, by the designation, and during the lifetime, of a predecessor. The tension between the claims to the succession of the caliph's brothers and those of his sons is, nevertheless, visible from time to time.

The accession of 'Umar II was unusual and remains somewhat puzzling. When Sulayman died the Umayyad army was engaged in a prolonged, and ultimately unsuccessful, siege of Constantinople (716–17). Sulayman's sons, one of whom he apparently first wished to succeed him, were either away at the siege or were too young, and on his deathbed he allowed himself to be persuaded by a rather shadowy religious figure at the Umayyad court, Raja' b. Haywa, to pass on the caliphate to his cousin 'Umar b. 'Abd al-'Aziz. Raja' then tricked the other Umayyads present at Sulayman's camp in northern Syria by getting them to give their allegiance to the person named as successor by Sulayman without revealing the name of the nominee. Subsequent hostility was defused by the promise that the succession would revert to the sons of 'Abd al-Malik, in the person of Yazid, after 'Umar's death.[1]

Whatever the truth about the way in which 'Umar's succession was achieved, it may be that it is to be explained as something of an emergency measure, to be seen against the background of the difficulties caused by the increasing demand among non-Arabs to be allowed to enter Islam and enjoy its benefits, difficulties which we have already noted in connection with al-Hajjaj's governorship in Iraq. Furthermore, it may be that the tensions thus arising were

72

increased by the protracted siege of Constantinople which must have required great expenditure without, in the end, much in return for the effort. However, one can only guess at the considerations like these which may have led to 'Umar's appointment, for the sources are not explicit about the reasons.[2]

The expedition mounted against Constantinople under Sulayman was part of the expansion and aggression of the Arabs and of Islam in the first two decades or so of the eighth century, not only in the east and the west, in northern India, central Asia and Spain, but also to the north against the Byzantine empire. Twice previously, under Mu'awiya, there had been attempts to take the Byzantine capital, and this third attempt under Sulayman represents the last attack by the Muslims on the city until Ottoman times. It was a major effort, on land and on sea, and was commanded by the caliph's brother, Maslama b. 'Abd al-Malik, whose own exclusion from the caliphate is usually explained by the fact that his mother was a non-Arab. Ultimately, the attack was unsuccessful, something which the early death of Sulayman, the accession of a new and vigorous Byzantine ruler in the person of Leo the Isaurian, and the apparent distaste of 'Umar II for aggressive policies, may help to explain. 'Umar probably gave the order for withdrawal, and the capture of Constantinople then receded into the realm of eschatological speculation until a later period.[3]

It is worth mentioning that Greek and Armenian tradition reports an exchange of letters on religious questions between 'Umar II and the emperor Leo, and the Armenian tradition even preserves what purports to be the text of the correspondence between them.[4]

The Family of al-Muhallab and the Development of Factionalism

The beginning of the emergence of the Mudari and Yemeni army factions in the east in the period after al-Hajjaj is associated with the career of Yazid b. al-Muhallab. His father, it will be remembered, had been responsible for the defeat of the Kharijites in Iraq in the early part of al-Hajjaj's governorate there. Consequently, al-Muhallab was made governor of Khurasan by al-Hajjaj in 698. He remained in office there until his death in 702 when he was succeeded by his son Yazid. Al-Muhallab and his family belonged to the 'southern' tribe of Azd, and the rise of Azd in Khurasan, where, as in Basra, they allied with the Rabi'a against the Mudar, is closely connected with the rise to power of the Muhallabids there. The family consciously promoted the interests of their tribe, perhaps because the Muhallabids themselves were of fairly obscure origin and wished to establish themselves among the leaders of Azd, and this may help to explain Yazid's partiality towards his relatives among the refugees from the revolt of Ibn al-Ash'ath who fled to Khurasan. We are told that he only rounded up the 'northerners' among them to send back to al-Hajjaj for punishment.

Relations between al-Hajjaj and Yazid b. al-Muhallab worsened and eventually, in 704, the Iraqi governor obtained the caliph's permission to remove Yazid from office and imprison him. In 709, however, taking advantage of the antagonism which existed between al-Hajjaj and the heir apparent, Sulayman, Yazid escaped from prison and took refuge at Ramla with Sulayman, at that time governor of Palestine.

The hostility between al-Hajjaj and Sulayman was connected with the former's desire for the succession to the caliphate of a son of al-Walid rather than Sulayman, but whether this was its cause or only a symptom is not clear. It is probably anachronistic to view al-Hajjaj as inextricably bound up with the 'northerners' while Sulayman was a supporter of the 'southerners'. Not all of al-Hajjaj's appointees belonged to Mudar, and in Khurasan Qutayba b. Muslim, who succeeded Yazid b. al-Muhallab, and who himself had no strong tribal backing there, found himself opposed by the Mudar even though he was regarded as al-Hajjaj's man. It has been argued that the Yemenis were generally in favour of assimilation with the non-Arabs and were opposed to an expansionist policy while the Mudar supported contrary points of view, and that the hostility of Sulayman and al-Hajjaj is similarly to be seen as a result of disagreement on these questions of policy.[5] Judging from what happened when Sulayman became caliph, however, it is difficult to see him as an 'anti-imperialist'. He, after all, launched the attack on Constantinople, supported campaigns for the subjugation of the Caspian provinces, and sent Syrian troops into Khurasan, apparently for the first time. It is true that some reports suggest that he reversed al-Hajjaj's measures that kept the *mawali* out of the Iraqi garrison towns, but one would hesitate, given the anecdotal nature of Muslim tradition, to attempt to describe Sulayman's rule as the pursuance of a complete political programme. It seems more satisfactory to see this period as one in which the factions were taking shape as the soldiers formed parties among themselves in pursuit of their economic and other interests, and individuals like Yazid b. al-Muhallab sought to use these for their own ends.

When Sulayman became caliph he installed Yazid b. al-Muhallab as governor of Iraq and the east, and Yazid appointed his own men, Yemenis, to the offices previously filled by al-Hajjaj's appointees. He persuaded Sulayman to let him govern from Khurasan, rather than from the usual seat of the governor, Iraq. The sources explain this as resulting from a desire to get out of the clutches of a financial intendant, a *mawla*, whom Sulayman had appointed with a small military force of his own to supervise the finances of Iraq. It may be too that Yazid foresaw greater opportunities for profit and the prospect of stronger support in the frontier province. In Khurasan, he led the campaigns against the Caspian provinces, which had been imperfectly subdued in the first wave of conquests, and it was during this period that Syrian troops were introduced into Khurasan. However, when 'Umar II became caliph in 717, he deposed Yazid and had him imprisoned, allegedly for too blatant feathering of his own nest while governor.

Either just before or just after the death of 'Umar in February 720, Yazid b. al-Muhallab escaped from his prison and fled to Basra where he was able to gain a body of support for a revolt. Possibly he knew what to expect under the new caliph Yazid b. 'Abd al-Malik who was descended on his mother's side from al-Hajjaj. In Basra the Muhallabids' own tribe of Azd was strong and, although the Umayyad governor was at first able to organise resistance against Yazid b. al-Muhallab, the resistance soon crumbled. This was partly a result of the rivalries among the different families and groups in the town, and partly because the governor was unable to match the material incentives offered by Yazid b. al-Muhallab. As a result, the latter took over the town and imprisoned its governor.

In his propaganda Ibn al-Muhallab is said to have called for a holy war against the Syrians and to have summoned the Basrans to 'the Book of God and the *Sunna* of His Prophet'. It is clear that he had some success in harnessing the religious opposition to the Umayyads, and among his supporters is named al-Sumayda' al-Kindi who is described as a supporter of the Kharijites. Although the basis of Yazid's support was his own Azdi kinsmen, he also obtained backing from many Mudaris, the more so after his capture of Wasit when he was joined by Mudaris from Kufa. It is not possible to align the supporters and opponents of Ibn al-Muhallab on a purely tribal basis, and, indeed, we hear that some Azdis were opposed to him. There seems to have been no Syrian garrison in Wasit at this time — it may have been withdrawn in connection with the siege of Constantinople.

From Basra in the summer of 720 Ibn al-Muhallab extended his control over Khuzistan, Kirman and Fars. In order to confront him the Umayyad army of Mesopotamia and the Syrian frontier was brought south under the command of Maslama b. 'Abd al-Malik. Now the religious element in the support of Ibn al-Muhallab proved a liability for, rather in the manner of 'Ali's pious followers at Siffin, it impeded the pressing home of any advantage. It was argued that the Syrians should be given a chance to accept the Book of God and the *Sunna* of the Prophet before they were attacked. In the event, when the fighting started towards the end of August the Muhallabid forces proved unreliable, especially the Mudar of Kufa who abandoned the field. Yazid b. al-Muhallab was killed in the battle and other members of the family fled as far afield as India. There, however, most of them were hunted down and either killed or taken captive until ransomed by their Azdi relatives.

The importance of the career of Ibn al-Muhallab lies in its intensification of the factional schism. His defeat was followed by the installation of Qaysis and other 'northerners' into the key offices in Iraq and the east, as a reaction to the identification of Ibn al-Muhallab with the Azd. To Iraq as governor there came a Qaysi, 'Umar b. Hubayra, a former governor of Mesopotamia. Furthermore, the army which put down the revolt in Iraq was the army of the Syrian-Mesopotamian frontier, and this was basically Qaysi in composition since its area of operation had been settled by 'northerners'. Previous Syrian troops in Iraq and the east, being drawn from south and central Syria, were predominantly Kalbi and Yemeni, and this may explain why there seems to have been some support for Ibn al-Muhallab among the troops of the Umayyad governor of Iraq. The defeat of Ibn al-Muhallab came to be seen by the Yemenis as one of their major humiliations at the hands of the Umayyads and one of the slogans of the Yemenis from Khurasan who helped the Hashimiyya to overthrow the Umayyads in 749–50 was 'revenge for Banu Muhallab'.[6]

'Umar II and the *Mawali*

We have already noted that 'Umar II occupies a distinct place in

Muslim tradition, and have attempted to offer some explanation for this fact.[7] While there is no doubt that the acceptance of 'Umar as a genuine caliph (*khalifa*), unlike the other Umayyads who count only as kings (*muluk*), is based to some extent on historical facts and on this caliph's personality and actions, it is also clear that much of the traditional writing about him should be regarded as pious and moralistic story-telling in keeping with the needs and outlook of tradition. Consequently, there is some difficulty in saying precisely what he did as caliph, let alone assessing his motives, and in any case, his reign was a very short one. Early western scholars tended to portray him as an impractical idealist, but following Wellhausen most see him as a pious individual who attempted to solve the problems of his day in a way which would reconcile the needs of his dynasty and state with the demands of Islam.[8]

Before becoming caliph, he had been for some time (706–12?) governor of Medina for his cousin al-Walid. He was removed from this post at the insistence of al-Hajjaj, who complained about his giving shelter there to subversive elements from Iraq. This association with Medina, traditionally regarded as the home of the *Sunna*, goes far to account for his reputation and outlook, and it is no surprise to find that some reports say he was born there (others say Egypt).

As caliph he is remembered above all as someone who attempted to solve, in a manner satisfactory to Islam and to those non-Arabs wishing to become Muslims, the problems arising from the fact that acceptance of Islam conferred fiscal privileges. Put generally, the problem was that Muslims did not, or at least should not, pay certain taxes to which non-Muslims were, or should have been, liable. This provided an incentive for non-Muslims to become Muslims, but the widespread acceptance of Islam then caused a decrease in the revenues of the government, so the Umayyad rulers had a vested interest in preventing the conquered peoples from accepting Islam or forcing them to continue paying those taxes from which they claimed exemption as Muslims. It is in this sense that al-Hajjaj's driving out of the *mawali* from the garrison towns is to be understood. 'Umar II, on the other hand, attempted to put into practice a system which recognised the right of anyone who wished to accept Islam to do so, gave them the advantages associated with the status of a Muslim, but went some way to preventing a complete collapse in the revenue of the government.

Difficulties arise, though, when we try to ask more precise

questions. How were non-Muslims taxed and how did they hope to benefit by accepting Islam? What did 'Umar do in attempting to reconcile the rights of the new Muslims (*mawali*) with the revenue needs of the government? How far were his measures effective and, if they were not, why not? The difficulties arise because the sources rarely supply the detailed and precise information we need, or if they do, the information may relate to only a limited area of the problem or a part of the Umayyad territories. There is too the danger that the information represents anachronistic reading back of later conditions into the time of 'Umar II. Even the lengthy and quite detailed so-called 'Fiscal Rescript of 'Umar II' is subject to these remarks. It has generally been accepted as a copy of a document sent by 'Umar to his governors giving them precise instructions on certain questions concerning taxation and the rights of non-Muslims to accept Islam, but it is clear from the attempt of H. A. R. Gibb to explicate it that it leaves a number of issues in doubt, and, in spite of the general acceptance of its authenticity, its ascription to 'Umar as a whole can only be impressionistic and open to question. Like almost all of our Umayyad 'documents', it survives only as part of a later literary text — there is no archive and we do not have the document itself, if there was one.[9]

If we take first the question of the taxation of non-Muslims and Muslims in the Umayyad state and the advantages to be hoped for from acceptance of Islam, it would be fairly easy, in theory at any rate, to provide an answer if the classical Muslim fiscal system had existed from the beginning. In this classical system Muslims specifically pay a religious tax, the *zakat*, which is levied at different rates on different types of property and wealth. Non-Muslims specifically pay a poll tax, the *jizya*, payable on the person of each non-Muslim, both as a sign of their inferior status in the Islamic state and as a return for the protection which this state offers them. Thirdly there is the *kharaj*. This is a tax payable equally by Muslims and non-Muslims on land which is liable for it, generally land which was conquered and became the property of the Muslim state but which was left under the cultivation of those who had worked it before its conquest, subject to a tax which was to be gathered for the benefit of the Muslims as a whole. When this land changed hands it remained liable for the *kharaj*, no matter what was the religion of its proprietor. In this system, then, there is likely to be some incentive for the adoption of Islam by the non-Muslims, so long as the financial burden of the *zakat* was less than that of the *jizya*, but the amount lost to the treasury by the conversion of an individual was unlikely to be significant for the finances of the state.[10]

In the Umayyad period, though, this system (admittedly more complex in practice) did not yet exist fully, and, largely as a result of the work of D. C. Dennett, it is apparent that we have to speak of fiscal systems rather than of one system covering the whole empire. Nevertheless, Dennett seems to have shown that, in spite of the diversity, there was at the level of the tax payer over most of the empire a dual system of poll tax and land tax, and a reasonably precise terminology to distinguish them. Acceptance of Islam should in theory have brought relief from the poll tax in most areas, but the land tax would continue to be payable so long as the convert remained on his land.[11] It seems, therefore, that the extensive effort made by Dennett to refute Wellhausen's picture of the Umayyad fiscal system does not lead to a radically different result. Full fiscal benefit would be gained both by conversion and by abandonment of the land, but it was abandonment of the land which was crucial since this freed a man from the land tax and removed him from the clutches of the tax official. It was this abandonment of the land which caused the problems for the Umayyads in both Egypt and Iraq, and it is against this background that al-Hajjaj's measures against the *mawali* make sense. Almost everywhere widespread acceptance of Islam would lead to a decline of revenue, either for the government where it collected the taxes directly (as in Iraq and Egypt) or for the local non-Arab rulers and notables charged with levying it and paying the government an agreed amount (as in Khurasan). To prevent this decline in revenue the government or the local notables, as the case may be, either tried to prevent conversion to Islam or took no account of it when collecting taxes. To this extent, therefore, Dennett's more sophisticated treatment of Umayyad taxation does not greatly alter the fact that there was a tension between the needs of the state and the demands of Islam.

It would be unwise to attempt to be too specific about 'Umar II's response to this situation. Beyond a general acceptance that there should be no distinction in Islam between Arab and non-Arab and that there should be no obstacles to acceptance of Islam by non-Arabs, it is difficult to pick out specific measures which we can be sure about. Some reports say that he forbade the acquisition of tax-paying land by the Muslims after the year 100 AH (AD 718–19).[12] This seems to indicate that Muslims did not expect to pay tax on their lands and as more and more tax-paying land passed into Muslim hands, either through its acquisition by Arabs from its previous non-Arab cultivators or by the conversion of its non-Arab cultivators, so the government was deprived of a vital source of taxation. There is a possible allusion to this measure in the 'Fiscal Rescript', but the wording is rather vague and there is no mention of any date.[13] It is reported that in Khurasan a deputation led by the pious Abu 'l-Sayda' complained to 'Umar that the governor al-Jarrah b. 'Abd Allah al-Hakami was imposing circumcision as a test on would-be converts who were flocking to Islam in response to 'Umar's insistence that the *mawali* should be freed from their *kharaj* tax and receive proper pay in the army. 'Umar's response was to depose the governor, forbid the circumcision test while insisting that 'God sent Muhammad to call men to Islam, not as a circumciser', and to demand that the non-Arabs entering Islam should receive equality of treatment with the Arabs.[14]

But whatever 'Umar did or did not do, it is clear that he did not provide a permanent solution to the problem, for after him we continue to hear of non-Arab Muslims being subjected to what they saw as unrighteous taxation, of consequent discontent and even revolt, and of renewed attempts by individual governors to recognise their rights. The problem seems to have been especially acute in the east where it caused constant trouble in the territories east of Khurasan, while in Khurasan itself we hear that in 738 thousands of Muslims were still taxed while many non-Muslims were getting off scot free.[15] Dennett argued that the dual system of land tax and poll tax, with remission of poll tax but not necessarily of land tax for those who accepted Islam, should have remedied the grievances of the *mawali* without injuring the interests of the state. But this works only if it is assumed that the system was respected, and then only in those areas where it operated. As Dennett himself pointed out, the system did not work in the east where the Arabs generally left the levying of taxes to local rulers and notables, insisting only on an agreed annual lump sum, and not concerning themselves with how or upon whom the taxes were imposed. When, therefore, as seems to have happened from time to time, an attempt was made to encourage the local population to accept Islam by promising remission of taxes, it was the local rulers and notables who came under pressure because they were the ones responsible for paying the agreed sum to the Arab governor. The Arabs were, then, in a difficult situation: either they supported the rights of the local notables and rulers and allowed them to raise the tribute demanded in any way they saw fit, or they supported the rights of the local *mawali* and made it difficult or impossible for the local authorities to meet the tribute demanded. The consequences appeared especially in events in the east during the long caliphate of Hisham.

Hisham and Khalid al-Qasri[16]

Hisham, the last of 'Abd al-Malik's sons to rule, had been designated by his predecessor, his brother Yazid II, who had also proclaimed that his own son, al-Walid, was to rule after Hisham. As one of the three longest reigning Umayyad caliphs, Hisham is the subject of numerous stories designed to illustrate his character, and overwhelmingly attention centres upon his desire for money. His rule is associated with tight-fisted and grasping financial policies. He is renowned for his acquisition and exploitation of huge personal estates, from which he derived great wealth, in this respect outdoing his governor of Iraq, Khalid al-Qasri. In the sphere of government he has a reputation for demanding massive sums to be remitted to Syria by the provincial governors, thus causing pressure to be put on the subjects and intensifying the problem of taxation and islamisation. His efficiency, however, became famous and it is reported that the 'Abbasid caliph al-Mansur, naturally no admirer of the Umayyads in general, singled out Hisham for praise on the basis of the tight control he exercised over the state finances.

In Iraq, the governor from 724, shortly after Hisham's succession, until 738 was Khalid b. 'Abd Allah al-Qasri. Sometimes his authority extended over the eastern provinces as a whole but on occasion Khurasan seems to have been removed from his jurisdiction and its governor appointed directly by the caliph. Khalid's family had been prominent in Syria almost from the start of the Umayyad period, and he had served as governor of Mecca, in the caliphate of al-Walid. Like Hisham, Khalid is well known for the wealth he derived from the landed estates in Iraq which he acquired. Hostility to him in tradition sometimes takes the form of accusations that he was an enemy of Islam and too favourable to Christians, Jews or even Zoroastrians. He is said to have remarked on one occasion that Christianity is superior to Islam and to have had a church built for his Christian mother behind the mosque in Kufa. He himself is sometimes called a Zindiq, a rather vague label which could indicate Manichaean or even atheistic leanings but which was often used polemically. His devotion to the dynasty was so great that Khalid is said to have declared his willingness to tear down the Ka'ba and remove it to Jerusalem if so ordered by the caliph. When he was governor of Mecca, it is said that he installed a supply of fresh water for the pilgrims and expressed his scorn for the sacred well of Zamzam and its bitter water, proclaiming the superiority of his water, provided at the instigation of God's deputy (the caliph).

Khalid's tribe was the Bajila, which does not seem to have been closely tied to either Yemen or Mudar and was not very strong in Iraq. His appointment as governor, therefore, may have been intended to diminish the factional rivalry there, which had recently been stirred up by the revolt of Yazid b. al-Muhallab and the succeeding Mudari regime of 'Umar b. Hubayra. If that was the intention, however, it seems not to have worked, for Khalid, as the supplanter of Ibn Hubayra, was perceived by Mudar as their enemy and identified as a pro-Yemeni. Yemen itself was less than wholehearted in accepting Khalid as its champion, but his fall in 738 and replacement by a Qaysi removed any hesitation which still existed, and in tradition Khalid is closely identified with the Yemeni interest.[17]

His period of governorship in Iraq seems to have been generally quiet, although in the year before his dismissal from office there was a small Kharijite outbreak in the north and a movement of Shi'ite extremists known as the *wusafa'* in Kufa.[18] Khalid had the two ringleaders of this latter group, al-Mughira b. Sa'id and Bayan b. Sam'an, arrested and executed. The execution of Ja'd b. Dirham, a rather shadowy figure associated with a variety of religious doctrines, is also sometimes attributed to Khalid, and these reports mention the strange detail that the execution was carried out on the Feast of Sacrifices (*'Id al-aḍḥā*) when Ja'd was substituted for the usual ritual sacrificial animal.[19]

By far the biggest event associated with Khalid's office was his fall from it in 738. The background to this is obscure, and the event is explained largely in personal terms in the sources, Hisham being said to have been jealous of Khalid's excessive land holdings. It seems, though, that Khalid's Mudari enemies were able to use their influence with Hisham to obtain a change of governor, and the first Khalid himself knew of the affair was when the new governor Yusuf b. 'Umar appeared in Iraq with orders that Khalid should submit to him. This he did and was led away to prison with his sons. He was to remain in prison for about eighteen months, undergoing torture as Yusuf b. 'Umar attempted to extract the fruits of his long period of office from him. This is the most celebrated example of a fate that was common for deposed governors in the Marwanid period. Eventually Khalid was released and made his way first to the caliph's court at Rusafa (Hisham choosing not to reside in Damascus) and then to Damascus. Here he lived on for a few years until Hisham's successor as caliph in effect sold him back to Yusuf b. 'Umar who again subjected him to torture, and Khalid died as a consequence of it.[20]

Under Yusuf b. 'Umar, a Thaqafi like al-Hajjaj, the tables were turned again and a period of Mudari domination of the east began. On the northern frontier the struggle with Byzantium was renewed under Hisham, having lapsed after the abortive attack on Constantinople in 716–17. The struggle took the form of constant raids and counter raids along the border between the two territories, and one of the participants on the Arab side, known as al-Battal, became the focus of a number of legends which were developed into something like an Arab Muslim saga. The traffic was not all in one direction and in 740 the Arabs suffered a serious defeat losing a large number of men, including according to tradition, al-Battal, on the field of Akroinos, possibly identifiable as modern Afium Karahisar.[21] At the same time slightly further east, on the western side of the Caspian, there was frequent conflict with the Khazar power of the north Caucasus which threatened the Arab possessions in Armenia, Azerbayjan and even Mesopotamia. On this front the campaign was led at first by Hisham's brother Maslama, but, after a major defeat at the hands of the Khazars in 730, the region was placed under the command of another Marwanid, Marwan b. Muhammad b. Marwan, the future caliph. He recruited a large army from the region and in 737 secured an important victory which ended the Khazar threat.[22] The participation of members of the Umayyad family as commanders in these operations on the northern front was important in that it helped to transform the caliphs from civilian into military figures, like the provincial governors. Thus far, although the caliphs had occasionally participated in campaigns before their accession, they had remained essentially apart from military affairs.

In the west, the best-known event of Hisham's reign is, of course, the Arab defeat at the hands of Charles Martel (Charles the Hammer) at Poitiers (also known as the battle of Tours) in 732. This came to be seen as the turning of the tide of the Arab advance into

Europe and inspired Edward Gibbon to a colourful passage in which he speculated on the possible consequences (muezzins in Oxford, Arab fleets on the Thames and Rhine), had the battle gone the other way.[23] At the time, though, a Berber revolt which broke out in 739 was more momentous for the Umayyad state. Having originally thrown in their lot with the Arabs, accepted Islam, and played a major part in the conquests in the west, the Berbers came, nevertheless, to be subjected to some of the disadvantages experienced by non-Arab Muslims elsewhere. Thus it is reported that 'Umar II found it necessary to suppress tribute demands which continued to be made upon the Berbers in spite of their acceptance of Islam. Possibly 'Umar had limited success for, under the caliph Yazid II, the Berbers murdered the governor Yazid b. Abi Muslim and installed a candidate of their own whom the caliph accepted. In 739, apparently again provoked by policies which denied them equality of status with the Arabs, and inspired by the egalitarian Kharijite teaching which had been brought from Iraq, they rose in revolt all over North Africa. Hisham had to send Syrian forces in an attempt to regain control, but when they arrived in Morocco in 741 they were severely defeated in battle on the river Sebu and the survivors had to flee to Spain for safety. In the next year the situation was retrieved somewhat when the governor of Egypt reestablished Umayyad authority at Qayrawan, but the tensions between Arabs and Berbers remained.[24]

But it was in the east, in the lands east of Khurasan, that the major military problems of Hisham's caliphate occurred, so much so that it is reported that when he was brought news of a victory he was unable to believe it, so used was he to receiving tidings of defeat. The area in question consisted of two territories: to the south and centring on Balkh, the province of Tukharistan (ancient Bactria); to the north Transoxania (in Arabic *Mā warā'a 'l-nahr*) or Soghdiana, with its capital at Samarqand. The population of both territories was basically Iranian but politically they were a patchwork of towns and principalities whose rulers used a wide variety of titles. Some of these rulers appear to have been of Turkish origin while others were Iranians. The territories had not yet been completely conquered by the Arabs to the same extent as Khurasan, but as a result of earlier penetration, and particularly of the conquests of Qutayba b. Muslim under al-Hajjaj, they had been brought into the Arab sphere of influence. Generally the more western areas were under the firmer control and regarded as more permanent conquests while the eastern parts were still relatively independent. The Arabs established garrisons in some of the main towns like Samarqand, Bukhara and Balkh, but the local rulers were left in office on condition that they paid a tribute to the Arabs. How they raised this tribute, by land tax or poll tax, was not stipulated.

Difficulties arose for the Arabs in the period after Qutayba's conquest from three developments in particular. Firstly there was the emergence, from 716 onwards of the Turkish tribes of the Turgesh under their chief Su-Lu, who, with Chinese backing, established a kingdom north-east of the Jaxartes (the Sayhun). This provided the local rulers of Transoxania with a counterweight to use as a balance against the pressure of the Arabs. Secondly there was the vacillation of the Arabs regarding the encouragement of islamisation and the desire to maintain the flow of tribute, contradictory aims. This gave rise not only to discontent and rebellion among the local peoples but also provided ammunition for the Muslim opponents of the Umayyads and enabled Arab rebels to find support among the non-Arabs and invest their movements with a religious colouring. Finally the growing factionalism among the Arabs themselves weakened their position.

The result was a long and complex period of generally unsuccessful military operations for the Arabs in the region, characterised by frequent changes of governor and shifts of policy on the question of whether or not islamisation was to be encouraged and the tribute lifted from the local Muslims. Khalid al-Qasri's period of office in Iraq began with a major disaster, the way for which may have been opened by a rebellion of the Yemenis in the army operating in Transoxania, known in tradition as the 'Day of Thirst' (724). The army was trapped by the Turgesh and rebel Soghdians on the far side of the Jaxartes, and the survivors only just made it back to Samarqand. After this event the Arabs found themselves on the defensive in the region and undertook no further aggressive campaigns there for about fifteen years.[25]

The vacillations in policy towards the non-Arab Muslims are best illustrated in the figure of Ashras b. 'Abd Allah al-Sulami, governor of Khurasan from 726 to 729 or 730. Allegedly on the advice of an Iranian secretary, Ashras tried to get the Soghdians to enter Islam by promising them equality with the Arabs if they did so. He sent Abu 'l-Sayda', whom we have already met as a proponent of the *mawali* in the time of 'Umar II, to Samarqand where, with the support of the local Arab governor, it was proclaimed that acceptance of Islam would bring with it remission of taxes. The result was a flood of converts among the local peoples, but also complaints from the local non-Arab notables and rulers that they were unable to meet their tribute payments now that so many of their people had become 'Arabs'. Consequently Ashras backtracked, demanded tests of the authenticity of the conversions (again circumcision is mentioned), and insisted that the taxes again be levied from those previously declared exempt. After the initial resistance when the local converts had some support from sympathetic Arabs, there was a general rising in conjunction with an invasion of the Turgesh, and most of Transoxania was lost to the Arabs apart from Samarqand and one or two less important places. Ashras's attempt to relieve the situation with an army from Merv in Khurasan resulted only in his being trapped in Bukhara, but eventually his successor as governor of Khurasan, Junayd b. 'Abd al-Rahman al-Murri, succeeded in rescuing him, relieving a siege of Samarqand and inflicting a temporary defeat on the Turgesh. The traditions about these events are, naturally, one-sided, and it may be that it was pressure from the caliph, rather than the local notables, which led Ashras to go back on his original policy. Gibb suggested that the local notables, in any case, were concerned not so much about meeting the tribute demanded from them by the Arabs as with preserving their own independence which they saw threatened by the spread of Islam among the local population. The way in which various episodes seem to echo those associated with 'Umar II is also worth remarking when assessing the reliability of the traditions.[26]

Arab sympathy for the injustices visited on the Soghdian *mawali* is connected above all with the movement of al-Harith b. Surayj. Al-Harith was a Tamimi (i.e., Mudari) Arab who led a movement both of Arabs (Mudar and Yemen) and of Soghdian *mawali*, supporting the rights of the latter as Muslims, opposing the Umayyads on religious grounds and demanding their acceptance of 'the Book and the *Sunna*', but willing to ally with the non-Muslim Turgesh in pursuit of his demands. This seems to be the first such case of Muslims willing to ally with non-Muslims against other Muslims. Al-Harith's movement lingered on for several years after its first appearance in 734, and eventually became entangled with the rise of the Hashimiyya in Khurasan. It may be significant that al-Harith is reported to have used black flags, later characteristic of the Hashimiyya and the 'Abbasids, but the meaning of these is open to question. Al-Harith is sometimes classified as a Murji'ite, as is his secretary Jahm b. Safwan. Murji'ism was an early form of Islam which stressed catholicity within the religion rather than the exclusivity which characterised, for instance, the Kharijites. It is, however, difficult to be sure of the exact nature of the religious doctrines of figures like Jahm who are associated with a variety of teachings in Muslim tradition. Al-Harith's movement appears to have been a particularly dangerous threat to Arab supremacy in Transoxania and even Khurasan. It may be that the sources tend to overlook the extent to which it was used by local dissidents and the Turgesh — Gibb stressed the way in which support for al-Harith melted away in the face of adversity — but we have little reason to cast doubt on the reality of the threat.

In 734 al-Harith took Balkh and marched into Khurasan aiming to capture Merv, the main Arab garrison town and seat of the governor. However, the newly appointed governor of Khurasan, 'Asim b. 'Abd Allah al-Hilali, defended the town successfully and drove off the attack, whereupon it seems that much of al-Harith's support melted away. Early in the next year, though, the revolt began again, and now the governor 'Asim, hearing that he was to be deposed from his governate, entered into negotiations with al-Harith and joined him in calling on the caliph Hisham to change his ways. The new governor of Khurasan was Asad, brother of Khalid al-Qasri, now appointed to the post for a second time. He succeeded, with his Azdi general, Juday' al-Kirmani, in driving al-Harith out of Khurasan and back across the Oxus where eventually he was forced to take refuge with the ruler of the Turgesh. Asad, meanwhile, transferred the residence of the governor from Merv in Khurasan to Balkh, capital of Tukharistan, possibly indicating his intention of giving priority to the keeping of order in the area and almost certainly because Balkh was now garrisoned with a recent influx of Syrian troops.[27]

The turning point in Arab fortunes in the eastern territories was the battle or skirmish at Kharistan in 737. The ruler of the Turgesh, Su-Lu, supported by al-Harith b. Surayj, marched into Tukharistan with a large army, but apparently failed to receive the local support which he expected. Asad marched out to meet him and came upon him at a time when most of the Turgesh forces were away on various expeditions and Su-Lu only had a relatively small force with him. Asad was able to inflict a defeat on the depleted Turgesh force and Su-Lu had to flee from Tukharistan, his retreat being protected by al-Harith b. Surayj. The expeditionary forces which he had despatched were not, however, so fortunate, and Juday' al-Kirmani was able to destroy most of them, only one band of Soghdians, we are told, making good its retreat. In itself this victory may not have been decisive, but on his return to his own capital Su-Lu was assassinated by a rival and the Turgesh broke up into contending factions. They never again threatened Arab dominance in Transoxania.

This was the victory about which Hisham was at first unbelieving when news of it was brought to him. Gibb emphasised the importance of Asad's decisiveness and his making of Balkh his capital in achieving it, and he underlined the importance of the skirmish. If it had gone the other way, it is likely that the local rulers of Tukharistan would have thrown in their lot with the Turgesh, Balkh would have been lost and from there eastern Khurasan would have been at risk. We are told that Asad ordered a fast to be observed in Balkh to give thanks to God for the victory. The defeat of the Turgesh was the major achievement of Asad's period of governorship in Khurasan, and in the next year, 738, he died while still in office, shortly before the fall of his brother, Khalid al-Qasri, from power in Iraq.[28]

As Asad's successor in Khurasan Hisham appointed Nasr b. Sayyar, a commander in the army there who had long been involved in the region's military affairs under Hisham. As it turned out, he was to be the last Umayyad governor of Khurasan.

Notes

1. C. H. Becker, "Omar II', *ZA*, 15 (1900), especially 21–5; J. Wellhausen, *Arab kingdom*, 264–6; C. E. Bosworth, 'Raja' b. Haywa', *IQ*, 16 (1972), especially 52 ff.

2. H. A. R. Gibb, 'Fiscal rescript', *Arabica*, 2 (1955); M. A. Shaban, *New interpretation*, 130–1; C. E. Bosworth, 'Raja' b. Haywa', *IQ*, 16 (1972), 70–5.

3. J. Wellhausen, 'Die Kämpfe der Araber mit den Romäern'; E. W. Brooks, 'The Arabs in Asia Minor (641–750) from Arabic sources', *Journal of Hellenic Studies*, 8 (1898); M. Canard, 'Les expeditions . . . contre Constantinople', *JA*, 108 (1926); R. J. H. Jenkins, 'Cyprus between Byzantium and Islam'; G. Ostrogorsky, *History of the Byzantine state*, English trans. London, 1956; H. A. R. Gibb, 'Arab-Byzantine relations under the Umayyad caliphate' in his *Studies on the civilization of Islam*.

4. A. Jeffrey, 'Ghevond's text', *The Harvard Theological Review*, 1944.

5. M. A. Shaban, *New interpretation*, 119–22.

6. J. Wellhausen, *Arab Kingdom*, 312–19; F. Gabrieli, 'La rivolta dei Muhallibiti'; M. A. Shaban, *New interpretation*, 136–7; *idem*, '*Abbasid revolution*, 93–5; P. Crone, *Slaves on horses*, 133–5, 141–3.

7. See above, pp. 15, 18.

8. On 'Umar's personality and career in general: J. Wellhausen, *Arab kingdom*, 304–11 (attacking the earlier views of Dozy, von Kremer and A. Müller); C. H. Becker, "Omar II'; H. A. R. Gibb, 'Fiscal rescript'; W. Barthold, 'The caliph 'Umar II', *IQ*, 15 (1971); C. E. Bosworth, 'Raja' b. Haywa', 72–3; M. A. Shaban, *New interpretation*, 131–5.

9. H. A. R. Gibb, 'Fiscal Rescript'; the 'document' comes from the life of 'Umar II (*Sirat 'Umar b. 'Abd al-'Aziz*), compiled by Ibn 'Abd al-Hakam who died in the mid-ninth century.

10. Articles 'Djizya', 'Kharadj' and 'Zakāt' in *EI*.

11. D. C. Dennett, *Conversion and the poll tax*; see too F. Løkkegaard, *Islamic taxation in the classical period*, Copenhagen, 1950.

12. J. Wellhausen, *Arab kingdom*, 286–91.

13. H. A. R. Gibb, 'Fiscal rescript', p. xiv and the corresponding note.

14. J. Wellhausen, *Arab kingdom*, 450–1; M. A. Shaban, *'Abbasid revolution*, 86–7; in the Arabic script the word for 'as a circumciser' (*khatinan*) is only distinguishable by a few dots from 'as a tax-collector' (*jabiyan*), and one more frequently finds the saying 'God sent Muhammad to call men to Islam, not as a tax-collector' attributed to 'Umar.

15. See below, pp. 106–7.

16. On the period of Hisham's caliphate in general see: F. Gabrieli, *Il califfato di Hisham*; articles 'Hisham b. 'Abd al-Malik' and 'Khalid b. 'Abd Allah al-Qasri' in *EI2*.

17. Cf. J. Wellhausen, *Arab kingdom*, 328 with P. Crone, *Slaves on horses*, 44.

18. W. Tucker, 'Mugiriyya', *Arabica*, 22 (1975); *idem*, 'Bayaniyya', *MW*, 65 (1975).

19. Article 'Dja'd b. Dirham' in *EI2*.

20. J. Wellhausen, *Arab kingdom*, 333–6, 358–9; F. Gabrieli, *Il califfato di Hisham*, 21–7.

21. J. Wellhausen, *Arab kingdom*, 339–40; *idem*, 'Die Kämpfe der Araber mit den Romäern', 444–5; E. W. Brooks, 'The Arabs in Asia Minor'; Tabari does not mention a specific place in connection with al-Battal's death, saying only that it was in the 'land of the Romans', but tradition attaches it to Karahisar, west of the lake of Akshahr. The tomb of al-Battal has tended to wander during the ages, however.

22. D. M. Dunlop, *Jewish Kazars*, 58–87; M. A. Shaban, *New interpretation*, 144–8.

23. Edward Gibbon, *Decline and fall of the Roman Empire*, chapter 52 (ed. Bury, vol. vi, 15).

24. J. Wellhausen, *Arab kingdom*, 343–5; *The Cambridge history of Africa*, vol. 2, London, 1978, 516–21.

25. J. Wellhausen, *Arab kingdom*, 454–5; H. A. R. Gibb, *Arab conquests in central Asia*, 64–7; M. A. Shaban, *'Abbasid revolution*, 106–7.

26. J. Wellhausen, *Arab kingdom*, 456–60; H. A. R. Gibb, *Arab conquests in central Asia*, 69–72; M. A. Shaban, *'Abbasid revolution*, 109–12.

27. J. Wellhausen, *Arab kingdom*, 464 ff.; H. A. R. Gibb, *Arab conquests in central Asia*, 76 ff.; M. A. Shaban, *'Abbasid revolution*, 118 ff.; article 'al-Harith b. Suraydj' in *EI2*.

28. J. Wellhausen, *Arab kingdom*, 467–74; H. A. R. Gibb, *Arab conquests in central Asia*, 81–5; M. A. Shaban, *'Abbasid revolution*, 121–7.

Chapter 7

The Third Civil War and the Caliphate of Marwan II

The third civil war,[1] designated as a *Fitna* like the first two, may be said to open with the rebellion against Hisham's successor al-Walid II in 744 and to end with the establishment of control by Marwan II over the central provinces of the empire in 747. Since it was followed almost immediately, however, by the outbreak of the movement in Khurasan which was to lead to the final collapse of Umayyad power a couple of years later, and since Marwan II's authority never had the same extent as that of earlier Umayyad caliphs, it is not possible to be precise about the chronological limits of this third *fitna*. The period was one of complex military and political turmoil and a breakdown of order. As in the second civil war, the Arabs of Syria were divided into 'northern' and 'southern' factions supporting different contenders for the caliphate, again the Umayyad family was split by internal divisions, again Kharijite and Shi'ite movements were able to take advantage of the situation to establish temporary control over fairly large expanses of territory, and again religious issues were entwined with the struggles between rival contenders for power. In spite of these superficial similarities, however, it is clear that the third civil war was not merely a rerun of the second, and that is why Marwan II, on emerging from it, was unable to establish his rule in the same way as had Mu'awiya and 'Abd al-Malik when they reestablished unity in 661 and 692.

Walid II

Although the deeper causes of the civil war are undoubtedly to be sought in the political, social and military developments of the Marwanid period as a whole, the immediate cause is portrayed in the sources in personal terms reminiscent of the earlier hostility between Sulayman and al-Hajjaj and its consequences when Sulayman became caliph. It is reported that the caliph Yazid II,

90

when he appointed his brother Hisham as heir apparent, had also specified that his own son al-Walid should be the successor to Hisham. This last, with the support of some members of the Umayyad family and other prominent Arabs, had considered overturning the succession arrangements made by Yazid II, in order to appoint one of his own sons as his successor. The designated heir apparent, al-Walid b. Yazid II, was himself a fluent poet with a reputation for loose living and lack of respect for Islam. After spending a lonely and embittered youth — he seems to have been eleven years old when Yazid II named him second in line for the succession in 720 — at Hisham's court in Rusafa (Rusafat Hisham, possibly to be identified as Qasr al-Khayr al-Sharqi in the desert north-east of Palmyra and not with the ancient Rusafa/Sergiopolis near the Euphrates), he later withdrew to a palace of his own in the Jordanian desert. Here he passed his time devoid of administrative responsibilities, awaiting the death of his uncle the caliph and his own succession. The plan to depose him was never put into effect but the intrigues involved must have soured al-Walid and marked out those involved as his enemies to be dealt with when power came to him.[2]

When Hisham died in 743 the agents whom al-Walid maintained at Rusafa immediately sealed up the dead man's property and brought the caliphal staff and seal, which we now hear about for the first time as apparently official caliphal regalia, to the new ruler. Al-Walid II received the oath of allegiance (the *bay'a*) in Damascus, but then withdrew to his own residence or residences (he is named as the builder of several) in the desert. The official protestations of joy on his accession brought to him from the provinces, the apparently genuine relief and fresh expectations felt at the death of the long-reigning and unpopular Hisham, and the goodwill acquired when the new caliph immediately increased the pay of those enrolled in the *diwan*, were all soon dissipated, however, and there shortly developed a plot to overthrow him. Three groups in particular were prominent in the opposition to al-Walid II.

Firstly, his measures against those who had earlier opposed his succession, including the execution of some prominent Arabs (although not members of the Umayyad family) and his flogging and imprisonment of his powerful cousin Sulayman b. Hisham, naturally increased the hatred of those already opposed to him on personal grounds. Some members of the Umayyad family, in particular the descendants of al-Walid I, the eldest son of 'Abd al-

Malik, were probably also incensed by al-Walid II's attempt to secure the succession in his own line when he appointed his own two sons as successors even though they were both minors.

Secondly, there seems to have been a religiously based opposition in the form of the Qadariyya or Ghaylaniyya, to some extent overlapping designations. The term Qadari has come to be used most commonly of those Muslims who supported the idea of human free will and responsibility for action in contrast to the more widespread view within Islam which stresses God's omnipotence and knowledge and therefore His predestination of events. It has been suggested that this essentially theological question had political overtones in that support for divine predestination might lead to quietistic acceptance of the political status quo, thus favouring the Umayyads, while support for human free will could imply the right of subjects to oppose rulers regarded as illegitimate. Consideration of the political activism associated with predestinarian doctrines in Reformation Europe does not inspire much confidence in this argument. This is why, it has been suggested, the caliph Hisham had taken measures against the Qadariyya and exiled their leaders to the Red Sea island of Dahlak. It also has to be said that beyond the use of the name Qadariyya we have little specific information about the controversy over free will and predestination in the time of Hisham, and in any case the sources are rather inconsistent in their use of the name, sometimes referring instead to the Ghaylaniyya. This name is associated with a certain Ghaylan al-Dimashqi, the Ghaylaniyya being his disciples. Ghaylan had served in the administration under 'Umar II but had later fallen foul of Hisham and was executed. He is sometimes called a Qadari but we know little or nothing about his beliefs and what information we have about the Ghaylaniyya points to views about the imamate rather than the free will *versus* predestination issue as such. It has also been suggested that the Ghaylaniyya supported those who wished to give the *mawali* equality with Arab Muslims and that Ghaylan's execution may have been connected with the contemporary rising in Transoxania of al-Harith b. Surayj, whose ideas and propaganda have something in common with those of the Ghaylaniyya. Individuals named in the sources as Ghaylanis or Qadaris seem to be *mawali* rather than Arabs. In any case al-Walid II is reported to have continued the policies of Hisham against the Qadariyya or Ghaylaniyya and consequently this group played an important part in the movement to overthrow the caliph.[3]

Finally the movement against al-Walid had a predominantly 'southern' (Kalbi and Yemeni) complexion, although there were Kalbis who continued to support the caliph while some 'northerners' (Qaysis and Mudaris) joined the opposition. In part the Yemeni opposition seems to stem from the background of al-Walid II. As the son of Yazid II, who had destroyed Ibn al-Muhallab, and with family connections with al-Hajjaj, al-Walid would have naturally aroused the suspicions of the Yemenis, and these suspicions would have seemed to be justified when he confirmed as governor of Iraq the Qaysi Yusuf b. 'Umar al-Thaqafi, who had supplanted the Yemeni candidate Khalid al-Qasri. Furthermore, apparently faced with an urgent need for cash, the caliph now delivered Khalid al-Qasri, who had been living in Damascus since his removal from office as governor of Iraq, to Yusuf b. 'Umar so that the latter could begin again the torture by means of which he was attempting to extract from Khalid the profits of his time as governor. This time Khalid died under the torture. The plot against al-Walid appears to have begun even before Khalid was handed over to Yusuf b. 'Umar, but this event intensified the Kalbi and Yemeni hostility to the caliph and, naturally, the sons and family of Khalid were also prominent in the opposition. Among the leading Kalbis named as supporters of the plot one of the most prominent is Mansur b. Jumhur al-Kalbi.

The opposition candidate was a son of al-Walid I, Yazid, who was to become Yazid III. Probably in April 744, after he had ridden into Damascus on an ass, possibly thereby hinting at a messianic status, his supporters were able to seize the town from the officials of al-Walid II, the caliph himself being resident elsewhere. Kalbi supporters from the surrounding districts, including a large number from the settlement of al-Mizza, known for its adherence to Qadarism or Ghaylanism, then flocked into the town. Yazid was now proclaimed as caliph and he received the *bay‘a*. Al-Walid II, after some hesitation, fled from his desert residence and took refuge at the fortified palace at al-Bakhra’ a few miles south of Palmyra, where he was joined by some Kalbis from Palmyra and Qaysis from Hims. Yazid sent a force against him there under the command of his cousin ‘Abd al-‘Aziz b. al-Hajjaj b. ‘Abd al-Malik. Lacking funds, al-Walid could not hold his relatively small force together and the Kalbis from Palmyra did not want to fight their relatives from the south. In the succeeding fight his men deserted in large numbers and he himself took refuge in an inside room of the fort.

There the attackers found and killed him, allegedly while he was reading the Koran like his ancestor 'Uthman when his house was attacked and he was killed, although this detail does not fit in with the anti-Islamic attitude which is ascribed to al-Walid II elsewhere. The head of the murdered caliph was sent to Yazid in Damascus for display while a piece of his skin was sent as a token of revenge to the family of Khalid al-Qasri. All this was in the same month in which Yazid had seized Damascus.

A rising of the Arabs of Hims, who had been supporters of the murdered caliph, was suppressed when a force marching on Damascus with the aim of installing as caliph a descendant of the Sufyanids, Abu Muhammad al-Sufyani, was defeated by Sulayman b. Hisham. Abu Muhammad was then imprisoned in Damascus along with the two sons of al-Walid II who had been designated heirs apparent by their father.[4]

Yazid III

The new caliph, Yazid III, occupies a rather unusual place in the list of Umayyad rulers on account of the righteous and disinterested attitude he is said to have had towards the caliphate. In this respect he is rather like 'Umar II, whom he is reported as taking as a model, although he is not accepted by tradition as a legitimate imam to the same extent as 'Umar II, only being counted as such by some of the Mu'tazilites. In his own time one of his supporters is said to have placed him above 'Umar II, for the latter, notwithstanding his many merits, was appointed in the autocratic way characteristic of the other Umayyads, while Yazid owed his caliphate, it was claimed, to the choice of the community. This estimate of Yazid, however, did not become generally accepted, and the man who is credited with expressing it was executed when Marwan II came to power.

The claim that Yazid had been chosen by the community in a legitimate way, unlike the other Umayyads, is based on his appeals for a *shura*. He justified his overthrow of al-Walid II by arguing that he had been calling for a *shura* but al-Walid II had used force to resist the appeals and he, therefore, had been forced to resort to arms to defend himself. This call for a *shura* is a frequent item in the propaganda of opponents of the Umayyads, associated, for example, with Ibn al-Zubayr and al-Harith b. Surayj, as well as with Yazid III. What it implied is not very clear, although the word denotes some form of consultation or taking of advice. The classic example of a *shura* in Islamic history is connected with the murder of the caliph 'Umar in 644. On his deathbed he is said to have allocated the choice of his successor to a *shura* and named six leading Muslims to consult together and make a choice from among themselves accordingly. It is questionable, though, what exactly later calls for *shura* intended.

But above all Yazid's religious attitude to power seems to come from his connections with the Qadariyya or Ghaylaniyya, whose attitude to the imamate he appears to have accepted. Since, in some respects, the Qadariyya were forerunners of the later Mu'tazilite theological movement, this probably accounts for the fact that the latter accepted him as an imam. On his accession in Damascus Yazid is credited with an introductory *khutba* in which he promised to avoid various abuses of power, implicitly attributing them to his predecessors, and concluded by stating that, if he failed to live up to his promises, his subjects would have the right to depose him if he did not respond to their calls to change his ways. Furthermore, if they wished to give allegiance to someone whom they thought better fitted for office, Yazid offered to be the first to give him allegiance and accept his commands. One should not obey a man in opposition to God; to God alone is complete obedience due. The connection of this speech with the programme of the Ghaylaniyya is indicated by a report which says that they held that the imam could be of Quraysh or any other family, Arab or non-Arab, that he was to owe his office only to his piety and his acceptance of the Koran and *Sunna*, and that the community has a duty to struggle against an unrighteous imam.

The list of abuses which Yazid promised to avoid may give some idea of the complaints made against the Umayyads by their opponents. He promised to cut back in building and irrigation works, perhaps indicating public resentment at the growth of private estates such as those of Hisham and Khalid al-Qasri; to spend the revenues raised from a territory only in that territory, perhaps a reaction to provincial resentment at the drain of resources to Syria; not to keep the soldiers away for long periods in remote areas, something which seems to have triggered the earlier revolt of Ibn al-Ash'ath; not to burden the payers of *jizya* so heavily that they were forced to abandon their lands and be unable to pass it on to their heirs; to give attention to the complaints of the weak against the strong; and to pay the stipends (of those enrolled in the *diwan*) regularly and equally, giving those living near at hand (the Syrians) no preference over those further away.

Apart from this proclamation in keeping with the views of the Ghaylaniyya, Yazid's caliphate is notable for a marked shift in favour of the Yemen, so important in bringing him to power. He removed Yusuf b. 'Umar al-Thaqafi from office as governor of Iraq and replaced him with the Kalbi leader Mansur b. Jumhur. After vainly trying to incite the Qaysis in the Syrian garrison in Iraq to resist the new governor, Yusuf b. 'Umar fled but was found in hiding in the Jordan area and then thrown into prison in Damascus. Mansur b. Jumhur appointed his own brother as governor of Khurasan, but Nasr b. Sayyar refused to accept his deposition from that office and, as things turned out, was saved by the course of events. Yazid was either dissatisfied with Mansur b. Jumhur, or changed his mind about the appointment, for after only two months he replaced him as governor of Iraq by a son of 'Umar II, 'Abd Allah b. 'Umar. We can only speculate about the precise reasons for this, but it may be a further instance of the influence of the pious opposition on the new caliph. Then, four months later, after a reign of only six months, Yazid himself died (September 744).[5]

Marwan II

Yazid had appointed, apparently at the prompting of the Ghaylaniyya, his own brother Ibrahim as his successor. He, however, seems to have received only limited acceptance and was faced with a revolt from the north led by a grandson of the first Marwan, Marwan b. Muhammad who was to become the last Umayyad ruler in Syria as Marwan II. Aged now between 50 and 60, Marwan had become powerful and experienced as governor of the northern frontier region of Mesopotamia where he had led the fighting against the Byzantines and Khazars. In the course of these wars he is credited with devising new military tactics and formations which departed from those employed by the earlier Arab armies. In tradition Marwan is sometimes called Marwan al-Ḥimār ('the Ass') or Marwan al-Ja'dī, both names for which a variety of sometimes not very convincing explanations are given.[6]

Already at the time of the murder of al-Walid II, Marwan seems to have considered a putsch. At that time he began to move south with his largely Qaysi army of the frontier, but had been forced to hold his hand by a mutiny of Kalbis whom he had left behind on the Caucasus frontier. He then seems to have accepted appointment as governor of Mesopotamia by Yazid III, taking up residence in the Qaysi centre of Harran and allowing the Kalbis who had caused him trouble to leave his army and return to southern Syria. With the death of Yazid, Marwan refused to accept Ibrahim as the next caliph and again marched south into Syria, winning support from the Qaysis of Qinnasrin and Hims. The leader of the Qinnasrin contingent was Yazid, a son of the earlier governor of Iraq and symbol of Qaysi suppression of the Muhallabids there, 'Umar b. Hubayra.

Opposition to Marwan's plans came from Sulayman b. Hisham, who had himself taken part in the wars on the Mesopotamian frontier and had built up a large private army of *mawali*, known, after its commander, as the Dhakwaniyya. Also supporting Sulayman were the Kalb of southern Syria. The two forces met at a point on the road from Damascus to Baalbek and Marwan was victorious. Sulayman's forces split up and he himself fled back to Damascus.

At this stage Marwan does not appear to have been claiming the caliphate himself, merely coming forth as the legitimist champion of the rights of the two sons of al-Walid II. These were still imprisoned in Damascus in the hands of Marwan's opponents and, whether or not it was the intended result, Marwan's insistence that the captives from Sulayman's defeated army should give allegiance to these two sons of al-Walid II led to Sulayman having them killed upon his return to Damascus. The killing is attributed to Yazid b. Khalid al-Qasri. Also killed at this time was Yusuf b. 'Umar al-Thaqafi, while Abu Muhammad al-Sufyani escaped and went into hiding. Thereupon Sulayman abandoned Damascus and fled, together with Ibrahim the designated successor of Yazid III, to the Kalbi centre of Palmyra.

Marwan entered Damascus and had the *bay'a* given to himself in December 744.[7] On the whole, apart from the battle with Sulayman b. Hisham, his takeover of power had so far been relatively peaceful, and the occupation of Damascus seems not to have had bloody repercussions for leading supporters of the previous regime, although some reprisals were taken against lesser figures, and anti-Qadari policies were again pursued. The generally peaceful intentions of Marwan were further displayed in his decision to allow the *ajnad* of Syria to choose their own prefects (*walis*) even though

Kalbi Palestine chose Thabit b. Nuʻaym, the man who had led the mutiny in the army which had prevented Marwan's first bid for power from getting off the ground. Marwan's hopes of a peaceful and secure start to his rule should then have been strengthened when Sulayman b. Hisham and Ibrahim, apparently seeing no future in continuing opposition, came to his court and sought reconciliation with him.

The new caliph did not stay in Damascus but moved his court to the Qaysi centre of Harran. This was a significant departure. It is true that earlier caliphs like Hisham and al-Walid II had sometimes preferred not to live in Damascus, possibly because, at a time when the plague was a frequent and deadly visitor, they thought it wiser to establish residences in the desert, possibly because of sentimental or aesthetic preferences for life away from the large town. But even in these cases the danger of absence from Damascus could be seen in the ease with which Yazid III had seized the town in his rebellion against al-Walid II. Marwan's move, which is probably to be explained by a clear-sighted understanding of where the real centre of his military power lay, however, went much further. For the first time a caliph seemed to have abandoned Syria altogether. Harran was not just the site of the court, but a real centre of administration and government, and although it could be argued that the move was a logical one given the changed conditions in Syria (see pp. 102–3), the Kalb of central and southern Syria, already suspicious of and hostile to Marwan, would hardly see it that way.[8] At any rate, there soon began a major rebellion against Marwan in Syria and, since Iraq had not yet submitted to him, his caliphate was for a time very precarious.

The rebellion in Syria lasted from 745 to 746 and may be divided into two stages. First, in the summer of 745, a revolt which seems to have begun among the Kalb in the south and to have been instigated by the *wali* of Palestine, Thabit b. Nuʻaym, spread to engulf most of Syria, including even Hims, which had been one of the centres most loyal to Marwan. This necessitated Marwan's coming to Syria and gradually reducing the dissident towns one by one, beginning with Hims which submitted after a siege, the Himsis apparently betraying the thousand or so Kalbis from Palmyra who had come there to strengthen the resistance of the town. From Hims, Marwan then relieved Damascus which was under siege from Yazid b. Khalid al-Qasri. Yazid's forces were scattered, he himself killed, and the Kalbi centre of al-Mizza put to fire. Thence Marwan relieved Tiberias, centre of the Jordanian *jund*, which was being besieged by Thabit b. Nu'aym. Thabit was subsequently again defeated in Palestine, taken prisoner and executed with his sons. Finally an attack on Palmyra led to a negotiated settlement with the Kalbi leader Abrash al-Kalbi. At this point Marwan seemed to have reestablished his position in Syria, and he took the opportunity to gather the Umayyad family together and appoint his two sons as his successors. Then, turning his attention to Iraq, he raised an army in Syria to go in support of the army of Mesopotamia which, under the command of Yazid Ibn Hubayra, was on its way south to enforce Marwan's authority there.

However, as the Syrian army passed Rusafa in 745 it revolted and Sulayman b. Hisham, with its support, made an attempt to seize the caliphate for himself. The rebels were able to take Qinnasrin, whose troops were on their way to Iraq under Yazid Ibn Hubayra, and were augmented by more Syrians eager to join the revolt. This forced Marwan to bring back most of the army from Iraq, leaving only a small force under Ibn Hubayra to continue the expedition. The caliph himself led the attack on the rebels and, near Qinnasrin, he was able to inflict a defeat on them, forcing Sulayman b. Hisham to flee via Hims and Palmyra to Kufa. Most of that part of Sulayman's army which had survived the defeat, however, remained in Hims under the command of Sulayman's brother Sa'id, and this necessitated Marwan's second siege of Hims, this one lasting for several months during the winter of 745–6 before the town finally fell. Marwan's anger at the continuing hostility of Syria following his fairly lenient treatment after the suppression of the first stage of the revolt now led him to raze the walls not only of Hims but also of other important Syrian towns including Damascus and, reportedly, Jerusalem. As Wellhausen expressed it, 'in the summer of 128 (746) he had finished with Syria; it lay in fragments at his feet'.[9]

In Iraq 'Abd Allah b. 'Umar, the governor appointed by Yazid III, had been confronted by a Shi'ite revolt in Kufa at the time of Marwan's takeover of power in Syria. This was led by 'Abd Allah b. Mu'awiya, not himself a descendant of 'Ali but only of 'Ali's brother Ja'far. Ibn 'Umar had been able to deal with the revolt in Iraq, using the garrison of Syrian troops now established in al-Hira, but Ibn Mu'awiya had fled to Istakhr in south-west Persia, from where he was able to control large areas of western Persia, attracting assorted discontented elements to his cause. Marwan, meanwhile, could only attempt to weaken Ibn 'Umar's position in Iraq by appointing a Qaysi in the Syrian army there, Nadr b. Sa'id al-Harashi, as his governor and hoping that he would be able to gain the support of the 'northerners' (Mudar) in the Syrian army. Nadr b. Sa'id established himself in Dayr Hind, a suburb of al-Hira, but the Kalbi majority of the garrison continued to support Ibn 'Umar in al-Hira. For several months there were skirmishes between the two, but then the appearance of a Kharijite threat reduced this contest between the factions in the Syrian army to secondary importance.[10]

This Kharijite threat had developed first among the Rabi'a tribes, technically 'northerners' but hostile to the Mudar and Qays, in northern Mesopotamia. Especially prominent was the tribe of Shayban. Their own appointed caliph, Dahhak b. Qays, gathered support among those soldiers of the Mesopotamian frontier who did not support Marwan and in 745 he appeared with a large force in Iraq. There he decisively defeated the rival Umayyad governors and while Nadr b. Sa'id seems to have fled to join Marwan in Syria, Ibn 'Umar and some of his Kalbis were shut up in Wasit. The spring and summer of 745 then saw the remarkable sight of the capitulation of Ibn 'Umar and his men, among them Mansur b. Jumhur al-Kalbi, to Dahhak b. Qays, their acceptance of Kharijism and of the non-Qurashi Dahhak as caliph (Ibn 'Umar, of course, was a Qurashi and an Umayyad), and the appointment of Ibn 'Umar as governor of Wasit, eastern Iraq and western Persia on behalf of Dahhak b. Qays. This appointment again brought Ibn 'Umar into contact with 'Abd Allah b. Mu'awiya. Here it should be remarked that in spite of their respective Shi'ite and Kharijite colourings, the movements of Ibn Mu'awiya and Dahhak b. Qays seem relatively flexible and able to absorb adherents of different viewpoints — one doubts whether Ibn 'Umar and Mansur b. Jumhur were fervent converts to Kharijism.

Dahhak governed the western part of his territories from Kufa but, probably in the spring of 746, he returned to Mesopotamia to take advantage of Marwan's difficulties in Syria. Occupying Mosul, his high wages attracted a large following to his cause, including Sulayman b. Hisham with those of his Dhakwaniyya whom he had saved from the earlier defeat at Marwan's hands. This was the time when Marwan was engaged in his second siege of Hims, but he was able to order his son 'Abd Allah, who was still at Harran, to prevent Dahhak's further advance. 'Abd Allah got as far as Nisibis where he was trapped, but Marwan himself, having subdued Hims, was now free to enter the field against Dahhak. In the ensuing battle at Kafartuta, Dahhak was killed and the Kharijite forces had to abandon Mosul.[11]

It was not until the next year, 747, however, that the Kharijites, now having chosen Abu Dulaf as their caliph, and on the advice of Sulayman b. Hisham having withdrawn to the eastern bank of the Tigris, were finally driven out and their threat ended. The stalemate which followed Marwan's victory at Kafartuta was ended when, after having established his control over Iraq, the Umayyad caliph was able to withdraw troops from there for use against Abu Dulaf and his men. Faced with this, the latter had to evacuate their position and withdrew through the mountains further east.

It was Yazid Ibn Hubayra who had finally established control over Iraq for Marwan. In the early summer of 747 he had defeated the Kharijite governor of Kufa, under whom Mansur b. Jumhur fought, captured the town and had then gone on to take Wasit and make Ibn 'Umar prisoner. At this juncture 'Abd Allah b. Mu'awiya alone remained as a focus for opposition to Marwan, and he was joined in western and south-western Persia by a conglomeration of disparate elements opposed to the Umayyad caliph — Shi'ites, Kharijites, Kalbis, Umayyads and even some 'Abbasids. The alliance, however, was clearly a fragile one and in 747 it suffered defeat at the hands of an army under one of Ibn Hubayra's generals. Ibn Mu'awiya himself fled to Khurasan, where he was murdered on the orders of the rising power there, Abu Muslim, who would tolerate no rival; Sulayman b. Hisham and Mansur b. Jumhur fled to India where they later met their deaths; the members of the 'Abbasid family who had joined Ibn Mu'awiya merely returned to their home in Jordan where they awaited further developments.[12]

Already before the defeat of Ibn Mu'awiya, Marwan had returned to his court at Harran, now having the most important provinces under his control. He may have been worried by the Byzantines who had taken the opportunities presented by the third civil war to extend their eastern borders. During this period too he had been receiving appeals for help from the governor of Khurasan, Nasr b. Sayyar, who was faced with dangerous developments in his province, but Marwan had been unable to heed such appeals. In fact the movement had already begun in Khurasan which was soon to destroy everything which Marwan had achieved and bring about the final ruin of the Umayyad caliphate.

The collapse of the Umayyad caliphate so soon after the close of the civil war, however, was not merely the fortuitous result of the fact that the rising of Abu Muslim and the Hashimiyya had begun at the same time. It seems clear that the civil war had itself been the culmination of changes which had been taking place in the nature of the state during the Marwanid period and that it brought these changes into the heart of the Umayyad caliphate — into its central province, Syria, and into the person of the caliph himself. While it was the rising of the Hashimiyya which finally toppled the structure, in part at least the developments which led to and were intensified by the civil war had already fatally weakened it.

In essence, the civil war reduced Syria to the condition of the other provinces. In the provinces, as we have seen, one of the main developments of the Marwanid period was the emergence and intensification of rivalry between army factions and military leaders. Syria, however, had remained aloof from this process because there the caliphs were in charge and the caliphs were not army commanders but a sort of hereditary aristocracy. Hisham remained as caliph whether power in Iraq was devolved to the Mudar or the Yemen. Under Hisham, however, some members of the Umayyad family began to be closely associated with particular military groups. Marwan was associated with the predominantly Qaysi army of the Mesopotamian frontier and Sulayman b. Hisham with his own private army, the Dhakwaniyya. At the same time, the Syrian army was developing into two distinct groups with the potentiality of the development of hostility between them — the predominantly Qaysi army of Mesopotamia and the predominantly Kalbi army of central and southern Syria which was sent to serve in Iraq, North Africa and other parts of the empire.

The personal and religious factors which subsequently triggered off the third civil war, the actions of al-Walid II and the religious and personal hatred which they inspired, then provided the opportunity for these developments to emerge fully. Yazid III was clearly supported mainly by the Yemeni faction and the religious opposition associated with the Ghaylaniyya, while Marwan came to power as the leader of the Qaysis. Unlike earlier caliphs, therefore, those brought to power by the civil war were clearly identified with one or another of the factions and this meant that the factional rivalry which had hitherto been confined to the provinces was now brought to the centre. In future the replacement of the domination of one faction by that of another would involve a change not only of provincial governors but of caliphs.

Furthermore, if Syria was now on a level with the other provinces, what reason was there for maintaining it as the capital province of the empire? Mu'awiya's rise to power had depended largely on the special conditions of Syria which had provided him with a united and disciplined army in contrast to those of his opponents, but now Syria no longer provided these advantages. Marwan's move to Qaysi Harran in Mesopotamia and his apparent transfer of the *jund* of Qinnasrin from Syria to Mesopotamia, while perhaps inspired by more short-term considerations, appears in the long run as a symbolic recognition of the loss of primacy by Syria.[13]

Notes

1. P. Crone, *Slaves on horses*, 46–8 for an overall interpretation.
2. On Walid II's upbringing and personality: F. Gabrieli, 'Al-Walid ibn Yazid', *RSO*, 15 (1935); R. Blachère, 'Le prince omayyade al-Walid (II)'; D. Derenk, *Leben und Dichtung*, 27–38; J. Wellhausen, *Arab kingdom*, 350–2.
3. Articles 'Ghaylan al-Dimashki' and 'Kadariyya' in *EI2*; W. M. Watt, *Formative period of Islamic thought*, 85–8; J. van Ess, 'Les Qadarites et la Gailaniyya de Yazid III', *SI*, 31 (1970); M. A. Cook, *Muslim dogma*, chapter 14, n. 30.
4. J. Wellhausen, *Arab kingdom*, 352–66; M. A. Shaban, *New interpretation*, 153–5; D. Derenk, *Leben und Dichtung*, 44–7.
5. J. Wellhausen, *Arab kingdom*, 366–9; M. A. Shaban, *New interpretation*, 155–60; J. van Ess, 'Les Qadarites et la Gailaniyya de Yazid III'.
6. J. Wellhausen, *Arab kingdom*, 371–3; article 'Marwan b. Muhammad' in *EI2*.
7. J. Wellhausen, *Arab kingdom*, 373–6; D. C. Dennett, *Marwan b. Muhammad*, 226–34.
8. J. Wellhausen, *Arab kingdom*, 378–9; D. C. Dennett, *Marwan b. Muhammad*, 238–9; article 'Harran', in *EI2*.
9. J. Wellhausen, *Arab kingdom*, 379–83.
10. J. Wellhausen, *Arab kingdom*, 383–7; article "Abd Allah b. Mu'awiya' in *EI2*; W. Tucker, "Abd Allah b. Mu'awiya', *SI*, 51 (1980).
11. J. Wellhausen, *Arab kingdom*, 387–92; M. A. Shaban, *New interpretation*, 160–2; article 'Dahhak b. Kays al-Shaybani' in *EI2*.
12. J. Wellhausen, *Arab kingdom*, 387–92; M. A. Shaban, *New interpretation*, 163; W. Tucker, "Abd Allah b. Mu'awiya', *SI*, 51 (1980).
13. P. Crone, *Slaves on horses*, 46–8.

Chapter 8

The Overthrow of the Umayyad Caliphate

Within three years of the restoration of Umayyad control over the central provinces by Marwan II, his power and that of his dynasty were completely destroyed. The agent of destruction was a rising which, beginning in Khurasan, was carried through mainly by Khurasanis and organised by a group known as the Hashimiyya. The result was the passing of the caliphate into the possession of the 'Abbasid family.[1]

Difficulties occur when we begin to ask questions about the nature and composition of the movement which overthrow the Umayyads, its aims and the reasons why it attracted support. These difficulties arise chiefly because the movement was necessarily secret in the years before its success, and as the historical tradition came to be stabilised in the period when the 'Abbasids were ruling as caliphs, the views of the new rulers and their relationship with Islam were changing too, making necessary a certain reformulation of the traditions about their rise to power and the bases of their legitimacy. There has been room, therefore, for considerable controversy over the nature of what is often called 'the 'Abbasid revolution', an expression which, if it has any validity, should be understood as referring to the many and profound developments which followed the accession of the dynasty, not merely to the overthrow of the Umayyads and establishment of the 'Abbasid caliphate itself. In recent years some new sources have been found which seem to throw more light on the Hashimiyya and its relationship to the 'Abbasid family in the time before the overthrow of the Umayyads. Although it is possible that these sources may have been evaluated too enthusiastically, they do contain some reports which were not available to earlier scholars like Wellhausen and which may help to clarify some of the obscurities.[2]

The Muslims of Khurasan

Although we do not have as much information as we should like about the situation in Khurasan, it seems clear that the reasons why a successful revolt against the Umayyads could begin there were that there was a large Muslim civilian population with grievances against the government, and that the Hashimiyya was first able to win support among these civilians and then to take advantage of the renewed factionalism in the army there following the third civil war. Distance from Syria and the problems of Marwan II in Iraq meant that, even if the caliph had been aware of the dangers, he would have been able to do little about them.

Nasr b. Sayyar had been made governor of the province by Hisham in 738, and, in spite of some difficulties, he had been able to maintain his position during the vicissitudes of the third civil war and was confirmed in office by Marwan II. This frontier district of the caliphate maintained an army drawn mainly from the local fighting men (*muqatila*) enrolled in the *diwan* and paid by the government, but including also from time to time troops from Syria. There was too, however, a significant non-military Arab popula-tion, earning a living in trade and agriculture, and more assimilated with the local non-Arab population than were the soldiers. Given the size of the province, the Arab layer of the population was spread relatively thinly, particularly outside the garrison towns, and this largely accounts for the lack of barriers between the civilian Arab settlers and the local Iranians. On the one side, significant numbers of the local population had accepted Islam, probably more than in the western regions of Iran, becoming *mawali* and taking Arab names indicating their tribal attachments. On the other, the Arabs intermarried with the locals, adopted their forms of dress, observed their festivals and probably used the local Persian dialect in everyday speech. As time went on, therefore, it became increas-ingly difficult to distinguish between the descendants of the Arab settlers and those of the *mawali*, and, although awareness of tribal origins and loyalties persisted, changed social conditions brought about a weakening of the tribal way of life and a consequent widening gap between the local mixed population and the *muqatila* bearing the same tribal names. The factionalism which split the Khurasani *muqatila* as it did elsewhere seems to have left the civilian population relatively unaffected.[3]

Apart from the opposition of the Yemeni faction in the army

towards the governor, there seem to have been a number of reasons for the development in Khurasan of opposition to the Umayyads. The province had been conquered and settled from Iraq, and there are some indications that the Iraqi opposition to Umayyad Syrian domination had been carried over to the frontier province. Shi'ism seems to have been strong there independently of the rise of the Hashimiyya, and this too might be explained as part of the Iraqi legacy — although not so important as Basra, Kufa had supplied some of the Arab colonisers in the province. Following the futile revolt of 'Ali's great-grandson Zayd b. 'Ali in Kufa in 740, his son Yahya fled to Khurasan in the expectation of finding support there, and a few years later he was followed by his relative 'Abd Allah b. Mu'awiya after his defeat at the hands of the forces of Marwan II. The close association of Arabs and non-Arabs in the civilian population seems to have inclined many of the Arabs to support the claims of the *mawali* and a universalist view of Islam, and to have increased the opposition to what were seen as the dynastic and unislamic policies of the Umayyads.[4]

The main grievance of the civilian Muslim population, however, probably resulted from the fact that they were subject to the authority of non-Muslim officials, and, particularly in the matter of taxation, felt themselves to be discriminated against to the advantage of non-Muslims. At the time of the province's conquest, the Arabs had made agreements with the local non-Muslim notables on a piecemeal basis enabling the latter to collect the taxes themselves so long as they handed over to the Arabs a regular fixed tribute. Under such a system it was natural that the non-Muslim notables would favour their own class or religious community, and it appears that this system continued almost to the end of the Umayyad period. The difficulties caused for the Umayyads in Transoxania have already been noted, and it seems that the situation was similar in Khurasan for it is against this background that the celebrated tax reform introduced by Nasr b. Sayyar is to be explained. The spread of Islam in Khurasan had made the old system obsolete, and, finding that many Muslims were paying taxes while a smaller number of non-Muslims were avoiding them, Nasr introduced into the province the system which was becoming established as the basis of Islamic taxation theory: all cultivators of taxable land, whether Muslim or non-Muslim, would pay the requisite land tax, while non-Muslims would additionally pay a poll tax from which Muslims would be free. This reform was made by

Nasr at the beginning of his period of office in 738, although we have no idea how effective it was or how long it took to be enforced. At any rate, it is likely that the measure came too late to defuse anti-Umayyad feeling in the province, and the question of taxation in any case has to be seen in the wider context of the development of Muslim opposition to Umayyad rule.[5]

The Army

Opposition to the government among the civilian population would not have been decisive in itself. It was only when it became linked with the factionalism in the army that the conditions for a successful revolt came into existence. The third civil war, with its intensification of the divisions within the army between 'northerners' and 'southerners', had its repercussions in Khurasan too. Marwan II had come to power as the leader of a Qaysi army, having overthrown the predominantly Kalbi regime introduced by Yazid III. The suspicion of the new government among the Yemenis (Azd and Rabi'a) of Khurasan came to a head in a dispute with Nasr b. Sayyar over the allocation of pay, and this was followed by a revolt of the Azd, led by Juday' al-Kirmani, against the government. The development of the factional division in the army under the Marwanids is illustrated in the slogan of the rebels, 'revenge for Banu Muhallab', a sign that the memory of past rivalries was not dead. The governor of Iraq who had overturned the regime of the Azdi Muhallabids in the time of Yazid II was, of course, 'Umar b. Hubayra, and now the new governor of Iraq for Marwan II was to be Yazid b. 'Umar b. Hubayra. Nasr b. Sayyar imprisoned al-Kirmani in Merv, but in the summer of 744 he escaped and gathered round him an army of Yemenis in opposition to the Umayyad governor.

At this stage al-Harith b. Surayj[6] appeared on the scene again. Following the failure of his rising in the caliphate of Hisham, Ibn Surayj had survived by taking refuge with the Turks. It now seems that Nasr b. Sayyar regarded the rebel as a possible ally against Juday' al-Kirmani. In the earlier fighting against Ibn Surayj, al-Kirmani had played a prominent part, and a number of the former's followers who had fallen into his hands had been severely treated. Furthermore, Ibn Surayj, although supported by forces from various tribal backgrounds, was himself a Tamimi (Mudar), and might be expected to oppose the Azd. Nasr, therefore, invited him to come to Merv. When he arrived in 746, however, Ibn Surayj, who had been joined by a number of his fellow Tamimis, attempted to take the town. He was not successful at first (his secretary, Jahm b. Safwan, being killed in the fighting), but he subsequently joined forces with al-Kirmani and together they forced the Umayyad governor to abandon Merv and flee westwards to Nishapur, a centre of the Qays (Mudar).

However, not surprisingly, the alliance between Ibn Surayj and al-Kirmani did not last. Some of the former's Tamimi supporters regretted that their backing for al-Kirmani's Yemeni rebels had resulted in the expulsion of the governor and his predominantly Mudari supporters. They soon, therefore, seceded from the alliance and were followed in this by Ibn Surayj himself. Fighting between the two former allies now took place, in the course of it Ibn Surayj was killed, and the Azd with al-Kirmani at their head emerged victorious.

With western Iran still controlled by Ibn Mu'awiya and the Kharijites, and Marwan II still struggling to establish his authority over Iraq, Nasr b. Sayyar's appeals for Syrian reinforcements went unheeded. Nevertheless, he decided to try to retake Merv with his own forces strengthened by the Qaysis from Nishapur. Returning to the eastern garrison town in the summer of 747, he and al-Kirmani camped facing one another outside Merv, each constructing defensive trenches. However, the preparations for conflict were hastily put aside when word was received that a revolt of a different kind had broken out in the villages nearby — this was the start of the rising of the Hashimiyya. Faced with this new threat, Nasr b. Sayyar entered into negotiations with al-Kirmani, but these were cut off when a son of al-Harith b. Surayj who was with the Umayyad governor decided to take vengeance for the death of his father by assassinating al-Kirmani. In spite of this, al-Kirmani's son and successor eventually concluded an agreement with Nasr, and in August the governor was again able to enter his provincial capital.

Abu Muslim, the leader of the Hashimiyya rising, now took action to turn the situation to his own advantage. We are told that he persuaded al-Kirmani's son 'Ali that Nasr b. Sayyar himself had had a hand in the murder of his father, and thus instigated 'Ali with the Azd who followed him to begin the armed struggle again. Both the Mudaris and the Yemenis now appealed to Abu Muslim for support. He gave it to the Yemen and when, early in 748, he marched into Merv with his Hashimi followers, Nasr again had to abandon the town and flee westwards. This time he was not to return.[7]

These circumstances help to explain the predominance of Yemenis in the movement which overthrew the Umayyads. It was not that the movement was a revolt of the Yemen against the government, or that the Yemenis had grievances not shared by others. But the fact that the area around Merv had been settled predominantly by Azd and other Yemenis meant that the activity of the Hashimiyya in the area was bound to attract a majority of Yemeni supporters, and when the revolt became entangled with the fighting between the Arab factions, it was the Yemeni opponents of the Umayyad governor who were eventually harnessed to provide support for the Hashimiyya in driving Nasr out of Merv. There was in fact Mudari participation both in the early agitation of the Hashimiyya and in the final revolt, but the location of the rising and local political circumstances gave both an overwhelmingly Yemeni colouring.

The 'Abbasids and the Hashimiyya

Al-'Abbas was an uncle of the Prophet Muhammad and a descendant of Hashim, the twin brother of the Umayyads' ancestor 'Abd Shams. Traditions about al-'Abbas are of questionable historical value since there were obvious reasons why proponents and opponents of his descendants' dynasty should want to put stories about him, for or against, into circulation. His son 'Abd Allah is a major figure in the sphere of Muslim tradition, where he is frequently cited as an authority on the interpretation of the Koran and legal questions. Again, it is virtually impossible to get a clear impression of an historical figure, but he is said to have been a supporter of 'Ali against Mu'awiya although after the former's death he became more neutral, even tolerant of Umayyad rule. It was not until after the death of 'Abd Allah b. al-'Abbas, in 687–8, that the 'Abbasid family appears to have developed political ambitions of its own.[8]

Around the end of the seventh century the family moved away from their home in the Hijaz to Syria and acquired an estate at Humayma in Jordan south of the Dead Sea. It may be that the move was connected with developing political ambitions, but tradition says that 'Abd Allah b. al-'Abbas, who had ordered the move before his death, advised his son to give allegiance to the Umayyad caliph, and it seems that the family was on reasonable terms with the Umayyads for some time after the move. In the Hijaz, it is reported, the 'Abbasids had been close to Muhammad b. al-Hanafiyya, that son of 'Ali who, perhaps unwittingly, became the focus of the hopes of Mukhtar and his followers in Kufa during the second civil war.[9] Whether or not this was true, it is certainly the case that the 'Abbasids later justified their own title to the imamate by the claim that it had been given to them by Muhammad b. al-Hanafiyya's son, Abu Hashim.

According to this claim, which was the 'Abbasids' chief justification for their rule until they abandoned it and substituted another around 780, when Abu Hashim was on his deathbed in the house of the head of the 'Abbasid family, Muhammad b. 'Ali, in Humayma about 717, he named Muhammad b. 'Ali as his successor. It is possible that this was just a story designed to give the ambitions of the 'Abbasids some justification, but it does seem in fact that the leading supporters of Abu Hashim's claims to the imamate in succession to his father transferred their allegiance to Muhammad b. 'Ali after Abu Hashim's death. The 'Abbasids indeed took over the party which had previously supported the claims of Abu Hashim and transformed it into one supporting themselves, and it is difficult to see how this could have happened unless the 'Abbasids had managed to convince the leaders of the party that Abu Hashim had transferred his claims to them.[10]

The movement which brought the 'Abbasids into the caliphate was known as the Hashimiyya. As we have seen, the descendants of Hashim b. 'Abd Manaf, the Banu Hashim, numbered among them the 'Abbasids as well as the Prophet Muhammad, 'Ali and their descendants. For some time, therefore, it was thought that the Hashimiyya was a sect which supported the religious and political claims of the descendants of Hashim, the most prominent of whom were the family of 'Ali. The 'Abbasids, more obscure descendants of Hashim, it was thought, somehow got control of this sect and used it to obtain power themselves although most of those supporting it assumed that they were working on behalf of an 'Alid. It now seems, though, that the name may not have been used in this sense until some time after the 'Abbasids had attained the caliphate and that originally it referred to the party which had supported the claims to the imamate of Muhammad b. al-Hanafiyya's son, Abu Hashim. After the failure of Mukhtar's revolt and the subsequent death of Muhammad b. al-Hanafiyya, it seems that some of those who had supported the imamate of Ibn al-Hanafiyya continued to support the claims of his son, and some Muslim writers on the sects of early Islam refer to this party as the Hashimiyya. The view that it was this sect which was taken over by the 'Abbasids is supported not only by the tradition of Abu Hashim's will in favour of Muhammad b. 'Ali the 'Abbasid, but also by some continuity of ideas and terminology between the movement led by Mukhtar and that which brought the 'Abbasids to power.[11]

From a later point of view it might seem odd that the 'Abbasids claimed power as the leaders of a movement which had begun as the party of a son of 'Ali and whose propaganda continued to stress relationship to the Prophet as a qualification for the imamate, winning the support of many who no doubt thought it was still working for an imam from among 'Ali's descendants. It is important to remember, though, that in the Umayyad period, although most of those who stressed the importance of relationship to the Prophet naturally looked for a leader from among the 'Alids, attitudes were not so exclusive as they became later. After the 'Abbasids attained the caliphate, most supporters of the 'Alids came to insist that there was only one imam in each generation and that he was only to be found in a line of descent from 'Ali through his wife Fatima, the daughter of the Prophet. Previously, ideas had been more flexible. Imams had been looked for in the line of descent from 'Ali through another wife, the Hanafi woman, as well as through Fatima, and 'Abd Allah b. Mu'awiya, who had rebelled against the Umayyads in the third civil war, had not been a descendant of 'Ali but of his brother Ja'far. In this situation it was not difficult for the 'Abbasids to stretch the concept of 'the family of the Prophet' a little more and say that they too should be included in it as descendants of the Prophet's uncle. When supporters of the 'Alids argued that the 'Abbasids were more remote relatives than the descendants of 'Ali, they replied that according to Arab custom the paternal uncles of a deceased man had greater rights of inheritance than the daughters — in others words, al-'Abbas, Muhammad's uncle, came before his daughter Fatima.[12]

The early stages of the propaganda (*da'wa*) of the Hashimiyya as the vehicle of the ambitions of the 'Abbasids are still somewhat obscure. At the time of the death of Abu Hashim the main centre of the movement was Kufa, but it seems that its following even there was rather small. Kufa continued to be the supervisory centre of the movement, although the 'Abbasid imams themselves remained in Humayma and its main activity was to centre more and more on Khurasan. From about the year 719 we read in the sources of missions being sent from Kufa to Khurasan to wage propaganda and recruit on behalf of the Hashimiyya, and from time to time we hear of the government in the province arresting and even executing propagandists who had come to its attention. Because the year 718–19 is the year 100 according to the Muslim calendar, and because the turn of the century is often vested with particular importance in Muslim tradition, scholars have been suspicious of these reports and pointed out that there is little sign that the *da'wa* made much progress in the province until some time later. A particularly important episode is associated with one Khidash who, at a date variously given between 727 and 738, propagandised on behalf of the Hashimiyya in Khurasan, was arrested and executed, and was then disowned by the 'Abbasid imam Muhammad b. 'Ali. It seems possible that Khidash was the first to win widespread support for the movement in the province, but there are some indications that he did not regard himself as a proponent of the 'Abbasids but rather of the 'Alids, and it may be that in his time the Hashimiyya in Khurasan had still not accepted the 'Abbasid takeover of the movement.[13]

In spite of the obscurities and conflicting reports, two points in particular seem to emerge. The first is that the *da'wa* used general and vague terms, and rarely, if ever, openly proclaimed that it was working for an 'Abbasid imamate. Typically the propaganda appealed for support for a member of 'the family' (*ahl al-bayt*) or 'the acceptable one of the family of Muhammad' (*al-riḍā min āl Muḥammad*); both expressions emphasised the importance of membership of the Prophet's family, and would be equally acceptable to supporters of the 'Alids and those with a more extensive idea of the membership of the family. The head of the movement in Kufa came to bear the title *wazīr āl Muḥammad* ('helper of the family of Muhammad'), while Abu Muslim, the leader in Khurasan, was *amin āl Muḥammad* ('trustee of the family of Muhammad'), both echoing titles used in the revolt of Mukhtar. The possible ambiguity of the name al-Hashimiyya has already been noted too.

Secondly, from the lists of names of missionaries and supporters of the movement it seems that *mawali* played a prominent part, but alongside Arabs, not exclusive of them. The significance of this is that some earlier European scholars saw the "Abbasid revolution' as almost completely a movement of non-Arabs attempting to overthrow Arab rule, or even as a revolt of the Aryan Iranians against the Semites. The evidence now, however, seems to show that this interpretation, which can be supported by reference to some Muslim sources, cannot be sustained. Rather we see a movement in which Arabs and *mawali* both participated. In fact, Arabs tend to be in the leading positions. The explanation for this participation of both Arabs and *mawali* is, as already suggested, that the Hashimiyya originally found support generally not among the soldiers but among the civilian population where the divide between Arabs and non-Arabs was breaking down.[14]

One other notable feature of the way in which the Hashimiyya operated is connected with the prominence in it of the names of *mawali* — the importance of names indicating that the bearer carried out a particular trade or at least belonged to a family involved in a trade. Frequently we meet individuals called 'saddlemaker', 'arrowmaker', 'druggist', and so on. Individuals with such names are nearly always *mawali*, and it seems that the movement was well aware of, and exploited, the ability of such men to move around unnoticed for the purposes of the *da'wa*. We have at least one report describing how a prominent member of the movement equipped himself with merchandise and took care to establish his *bona fides* as a merchant while his real aim was to work on behalf of the movement. In this way, as in others, we gain the impression of a cleverly organised and clear-sighted group, aware of the need for secrecy and the importance of winning as many different sources of support as possible for the cause.[15]

Following the affair of Khidash, leadership of the Hashimiyya in Khurasan was assumed by a Yemeni Arab of Khuza'a, Sulayman b. Kathir. He, it seems, was chosen by the movement in Khurasan and not appointed either by the imam Muhammad b. 'Ali or by the head of the Hashimiyya in Kufa. For some time he continued to maintain the independence of the Khurasani Hashimiyya, and it was only gradually that the movement there came to accept 'Abbasid tutelage. It may be that the decisive event was the capture and execution of the 'Alid Yahya b. Zayd by Nasr b. Sayyar in 743, which may have illustrated that the 'Abbasids were the only realistic contenders for power. In the same year Muhammad b. 'Ali died and was succeeded as putative imam by his son Ibrahim, and shortly afterwards control of the organisation of the *da'wa* in Kufa was given to Abu Salama. All of these changes seem to have improved the relations between the Khurasani Hashimiyya, the Kufan organisation, and the 'Abbasid imam, but still the Khurasanis appeared unwilling to act merely as the servants of others. This should not be regarded as surprising because by this time the movement in Khurasan must have been bigger and more important than that in Kufa. In Khurasan it was not confined to the area of Merv, but had branches in various other parts of the province, and we hear of a leading group of 12 *nuqaba'* (heads) and 70 *du'at* (propagandists) who ran it.[16] It was the appointment of Abu Muslim as his personal representative in Khurasan by the imam Ibrahim which finally ensured that the Khurasani Hashimiyya would work for the 'Abbasids.

Traditions about the origins of Abu Muslim are vague and sometimes contradictory, and it is reported that he himself discouraged enquiries about his antecedents, stressing that he was a Muslim who had identified himself with Khurasan (he was probably not born there) and that was all that was needed to be known. After the 'Abbasids had gained power he continued to have a large personal following in Khurasan especially, and his breach with, and subsequent death on the orders of, the 'Abbasid caliph al-Mansur meant that there were additional reasons for the further elaboration of his image by his supporters and opponents. It is difficult, there-fore, to say anything certain about him before he came into contact with the Hashimiyya in Kufa, attracted the attention of the head of the propaganda there, Abu Salama, and was subsequently taken up by the imam Ibrahim who made him his *mawla*. It was this last event which made it possible for Abu Muslim to be referred to as one of 'the family' (*ahl al-bayt*).

After sending him as his personal messenger to the *da'wa* in Khurasan on a number of occasions, Ibrahim finally sent him there to take over the leadership of the Hashimiyya in the province. The date and circumstances are variously reported. It is not clear whether it was in 746 or 747, whether the Khurasanis had asked Ibrahim to send them a leader or whether Ibrahim sent him with the aim of imposing his control over the Hashimiyya and suppressing local tendencies to independence. At any rate it seems that Sulayman b. Kathir, the leader of the Hashimiyya in the Merv area at that time, was unwilling to accept Abu Muslim's suzerainty, but the latter was able to exploit divisions within the Hashimiyya to establish his own position, even though Sulayman continued to be important for some time; Abu Muslim was only able to deal with him finally, having him killed, after the overthrow of the Umayyads had been achieved.[17]

It was the summer of 747 that the open revolt of the Hashimiyya began with the unfurling of the black flags which had been sent to Khurasan by the imam Ibrahim, in the village of Sikadanj near Merv. Sikadanj belonged to the Yemeni Khuza'a and was the dwelling place of the Khuza'i Sulayman b. Kathir. It was he who led the first prayer service on behalf of the 'Abbasid imam, possibly on the great feast which marks the end of the Muslim month of fasting in Ramadan. Moving around among the villages outside Merv, Abu Muslim was able to raise a force of some size, and we are told that he entered their names on a new *diwan*, according to their place of origin, not, as was the Umayyad practice, according to tribal attachment. It was at this juncture that the army factions in Merv attempted to compose their quarrel and even sent a force against the Hashimiyya, but Abu Muslim was able to repel it without much difficulty. Having reopened the divisions between Mudar and Yemen in Merv by means already mentioned, and after a period in which his support was sought by both factions, Abu Muslim came out in favour of the Yemen and was able to enter Merv at the head of his own men. This was most probably early in 748. On the following day Nasr b. Sayyar abandoned the town.

Even at this late stage, it seems, the allegiance of the Hashimiyya to the 'Abbasids was not widely proclaimed, and the oath of allegiance administered after the entry into Merv continued to talk vaguely of *al-riḍā min āl Muḥammad*. To what extent the Yemeni faction in the town, led by 'Ali b. Juday' al-Kirmani, now made common cause with the Hashimiyya forces is not entirely clear, but it seems that the two forces were not merged and it may be that for some time 'Ali al-Kirmani saw himself as making use of Abu Muslim for his own ends. Soon, however, it was clear that Abu Muslim was the dominant figure, and he was able to dispatch the forces of the Hashimiyya under the command of Qahtaba b. Shabib al-Ta'i westwards in pursuit of Nasr b. Sayyar.[18]

The Umayyad Collapse

Qahtaba had been in Mecca, where he met the imam Ibrahim, while the Hashimiyya had moved into Merv. He had been designated by the imam as military commander of the forces of the Hashimiyya, and when he returned to Merv it appears that Abu Muslim willingly accepted the appointment. Qahtaba and his son al-Hasan were to lead the campaigns which overthrew the Umayyads. They were Yemenis like many, but not all, of the Arabs prominent in the Khurasani army.[19]

By the end of June 748, Nasr b. Sayyar, having failed to repulse the Khurasani army, had to abandon Nishapur and withdraw west to Qumis on the border between Khurasan and Jurjan. Here he was joined, at last, by an Umayyad army sent from Iraq on the orders of the caliph Marwan II himself, but there was insufficient co-operation between the commander of the reinforcements and Nasr, and, at the beginning of August, Qahtaba defeated the newly arrived army and killed its commander. Nasr, who had been successfully holding out in Qumis against Qahtaba's son al-Hasan now had to abandon the area, fleeing west to Hamadan. It was there, by now an old and defeated man, that the last Umayyad governor of Khurasan died.

Meanwhile, Abu Muslim had definitively asserted his superiority over the Yemenis of Merv. For a time he had worked, it seems, in uneasy alliance with 'Ali b. Juday' al-Kirmani, and 'Ali's brother 'Uthman was sent to Balkh as governor while the new regime was struggling to assert itself in Transoxania. Apparently 'Uthman did not have much success in this role and the man eventually responsible for nullifying opposition in Transoxania was Abu Muslim's close associate, an Arab of Rabi'a, Abu Da'ud al-Bakri. Now, while Qahtaba was driving Nasr b. Sayyar from Nishapur, Abu Muslim, evidently regarding the alliance as having served its purpose, had 'Ali al-Kirmani and his brother killed.

From Qumis, Qahtaba moved west, taking Rayy and Hamadan without difficulty. At Nihawand, however, the Umayyad forces from Hamadan, together with those which had followed Nasr b. Sayyar, made a stand and were besieged by Qahtaba's son. A relieving Syrian army was defeated by Qahtaba and the siege continued for two or three months until finally the Syrians in the town agreed to make terms with the Hashimiyya forces, leaving the Khurasani followers of Nasr to be put to death.

The way to Iraq was now open. Qahtaba, heading for Kufa, avoided the army of the governor Yazid b. 'Umar b. Hubayra, but when Ibn Hubayra finally caught up with him the Khurasanis mounted a surprise night attack and the Iraqi governor and his men were forced to take refuge in Wasit. Bottled up there, they were effectively out of action and could be left to be dealt with when the opportunity arose. In the night attack, however, Qahtaba had lost his life. This was in August 749.

Command of the Khurasanis now passed to al-Hasan b. Qahtaba and it was he who, taking advantage of a pro-'Abbasid rebellion in Kufa when Muhammad b. Khalid al-Qasri seized the citadel with Yemeni support, entered the Iraqi garrison town on 2 September. Abu Salama, the head of the *da'wa* there, now appears to have attempted to take control of affairs into his own hands. The Khurasanis were camped at Hammam A'yan outside Kufa and Abu Salama joined them there. In the turmoil of the preceding months the imam Ibrahim had been imprisoned in Harran by Marwan II and seems to have been killed there, although the circumstances are obscure. It is said that he named his brother Abu'l-'Abbas as his successor and, on the fall of Kufa, he and other leading members of the family made his way there. Abu Salama now, however, was reluctant to recognise the authority of any of the members of the 'Abbasid family and intended to recognize an 'Alid as imam. To this end he kept the arrival of the 'Abbasids in Kufa secret. Abu Muslim's representative with the army was a certain Abu Jahm and he, it seems, got wind of what was happening and informed the Khurasanis. Thereupon twelve of the army leaders rode into Kufa, sought out Abu'l-'Abbas and gave him the *bay'a* as caliph. Abu Salama, out on a limb, could not refuse to do likewise. On the following day, Friday 28 November 749, Abu'l-'Abbas was publicly recognised as caliph in the mosque of Kufa.

Following the fall of Nihawand, Qahtaba had sent Abu 'Awn al-Azdi to establish control over the area around Mosul. There he was joined by the 'Abbasid 'Abd Allah b. 'Ali who effectively took command. The Umayyad caliph Marwan II was now drawn into battle from Harran. With an army of Mesopotamians and Syrians he advanced to met the 'Abbasid force but in January 750, at what is known as the battle of the Greater Zab, a tributary of the Tigris on its left bank, Marwan was defeated and his army destroyed. All he could do was to flee with the 'Abbasid forces in hot pursuit. Moving south through Syria, he could find no refuge and had to retire to Egypt. Behind him the Syrian towns submitted to the 'Abbasids, only Damascus offering much resistance. When it fell in April 750 'Abd Allah b. 'Ali sent his brother Salih together with Abu 'Awn and a small force to Egypt to track Marwan down. At Busir in Egypt he was at last caught with his small group of remaining supporters, killed, and his head sent back to Abu'l-'Abbas. This was in August 750.

It remained only to put the seal on the 'Abbasid victory. Ibn Hubayra in Wasit surrendered on terms when news of Marwan's death arrived, but the terms were dishonoured and he and the Mudaris in the garrison were all killed. In Syria the tombs of the Umayyads, with the exception of 'Umar II, were violated, with particular venom being shown to the remains of Hisham. In various places members of the Umayyad family were rounded up and killed, only those who went into hiding escaping. One who did survive was a grandson of Hisham who eventually made his way to Spain, found support there and established an Umayyad dynasty which was to last until the eleventh century. In Syria and the east, though, the first dynasty of Islamic history was at an end.[20]

Notes

1. The bibliography on the so-called 'Abbasid revolution is relatively extensive. In addition to what follows see H. Kennedy, *Early Abbasid caliphate*; article "Abbasids' in *EI2*; C. Cahen, 'Points de vue'; T. Nagel, *Entstehung des abbasidischen Kalifates*.

2. See M. Sharon, 'The 'Abbasid *da'wa* reexamined'; *idem*, *Black banners*, especially 231–8; F. Omar, *'Abbasid caliphate*, 16 ff.; A. A. Duri, *Daw' jadid*.

3. J. Wellhausen, *Arab kingdom*, 397–491 (on the development of the factions), 492–9; M. A. Shaban, *'Abbasid revolution*, 114–18; M. Sharon, *Black banners*, 65–71.

4. J. Wellhausen, *Arab kingdom*, 499–506; M. Sharon, *Black banners*, 54–65; article 'Zayd b. 'Ali' in *EI1*; on 'Abd Allah b. Mu'awiya, see above, pp. 99–101.

5. J. Wellhausen, *Arab kingdom*, 477–82; D. C. Dennett, *Conversion and the poll tax*, 124 ff.; M. A. Shaban, *'Abbasid revolution*, 129–31.

6. On him, see above, pp. 86–8.

7. J. Wellhausen, *Arab kingdom*, 482–91; M. A. Shaban, *'Abbasid revolution*, 131–7.

8. Articles 'al-'Abbas b. 'Abd al-Muttalib' and "Abd Allah b. al-'Abbas' in *EI2*; M. Sharon, *Black banners*, 93–9.

9. M. Sharon, *Black banners*, 111–21.

10. Article "Abbasids' in *EI2*; J. Wellhausen, *Arab kingdom*, 501–6; S. Moscati, 'Il testamento di Abu Hasim', *RSO* (1952); M. Sharon, *Black banners*, 121 ff.

11. M. A. Shaban, *'Abbasid revolution*, 138 ff.; M. Sharon, *Black banners*, 103–51.

12. M. Sharon, *Black banners*, 75–93.

13. J. Wellhausen, *Arab kingdom*, 514–18; M. Sharon, *Black banners*, 165–73.

14. Wellhausen's analysis of the ethnic composition of the Hashimiyya movement seems more subtle than some recent writers have suggested: *Arab kingdom*, 494–8, 513–15, 534–6; cf. M. A. Shaban, *'Abbasid revolution*, 155–8. The latter's suggestion that Suqadim in the sources should be amended to read *taqādum* has not received much support.

15. J. Wellhausen, *Arab kingdom*, 506–18; M. Sharon, *Black banners*, 155–73.
16. F. Omar, *'Abbasid caliphate*, 88–92; M. Sharon, *Black banners*, 186–200.
17. J. Wellhausen, *Arab kingdom*, 518–22; R. N. Frye, 'The role of Abu Muslim', *MW*, 37 (1947); M. A. Shaban, *'Abbasid revolution*, 153–55; M. Sharon, *Black banners*, 203–26; article 'Abu Muslim' in *EI2*.
18. J. Wellhausen, *Arab kingdom*, 522–36.
19. Article 'Kahtaba b. Shabib' in *EI2*.
20. On the victorious campaigns of the Hashimiyya armies, the destruction of the Umayyad and establishment of the 'Abbasid dynasties, see J. Wellhausen, *Arab kingdom*, 539–66.

Appendix 1

A Note on the Sources

Any history of the Umayyad caliphate which aims to do more than supply a bare outline of the succession of the caliphs and most important governors has to rely above all on the literature produced in Arabic by Muslims and established in the form in which it has come down to us some time after the dynasty had disappeared. The attitude of these Muslim literary sources to the Umayyads, the way in which they were compiled, and the difficulties arising from the comparatively late redactions in which we have them, have been discussed in chapter 1 under the subheading 'The Umayyads in Muslim Tradition'. This note is only intended to supply some indication of the more important authors and their works.

Muslim literary sources may be divided into several categories, according to their titles and their methods of organising their material. However, to some extent the diversity produced by this method of categorisation is illusory, since one often finds the same basic material in works whose titles lead one to classify them as different literary genres.

Among the chronicles (the titles of which frequently use the word *ta'rikh*), the fullest and most detailed by far of the early works is that of Tabari (d. 923). It was the European edition of Tabari's work in the later part of the nineteenth century which, running to 15 volumes, made it possible for Wellhausen to put Umayyad history on a new footing in his *Arab kingdom and its fall*. Other notable early chronicles are that of al-Ya'qubi (d. 897), which is relatively more pro-Shi'ite in flavour, and, for the later Umayyad period, an anonymous eleventh-century chronicle edited by M. J. de Goeje in his *Fragmenta Historicorum Arabicorum*.

Biographies of prominent figures of the Umayyad period are usually contained in collections, organised according to different principles, such as the *Ansab al-ashraf* of Baladhuri (d. 892), the

120

Tabaqat of Ibn Sa'd (d. 845) or the *Ta'rikh madinat Dimashq* of Ibn 'Asakir (d. 1176), which is a biographical dictionary in spite of its title. 'Umar II, unusually, was the subject of an individual early biographical treatment by Ibn 'Abd al-Hakam (d. 870).

In works written on the theme of the Arab conquests (*futuh*), such as the *Futuh al-buldan* of Baladhuri, the *Futuh Misr* of Ibn 'Abd al-Hakam, and the *Kitab al-Futuh* of Ibn A'tham al-Kufi (fl. early ninth century) one also finds a wealth of material relevant for Umayyad history.

Poetry from the period by poets such as Farazdaq and Jarir (both died about 730) is perhaps not so explicitly informative for historical purposes as we would like, but the collection of verses and biographical information about poets, the *Kitab al-Aghani* by Abu'l-Faraj al-Isfahani (d. 967), contains much of value for the history of the period in general.

For the development of the Shi'a and the Kharijites and the host of sub-sects, there is a tradition of heresiographical works, in which the beliefs, practices and main personalities are described. One of the earliest was the *Maqalat al-islamiyyin* of al-Ash'ari (d. 935).

One could continue to list such material for some time, for there is certainly no shortage of it. Works in these genres and others continued to be produced by Muslims down to modern times, and one frequently finds material relevant for the Umayyad period, not contained in the early writings, in relatively late works. The problem, as has been stressed, is what reliance is to be placed on Muslim literary sources in general, sources which from one point of view are all secondary, in that they are produced at a late date on the basis of material which has disappeared, but which are primary in that we have nothing earlier to give us comparable detail on the period.

Source material produced in the Umayyad period itself consists of some literature produced by non-Arabs in languages such as Syriac and Armenian, coins, inscriptions, buildings and other artifacts, and the administrative documents on papyrus which have survived. On these in general see the 'Index of sources' in M. A. Cook and P. Crone, *Hagarism*; on Syriac sources, S. P. Brock, 'Syriac sources for seventh century history'; on numismatics, J. Walker, *Catalogue of the Arab-Byzantine and post-reform Umaiyad coins*, and *Catalogue of the Arab-Sasanian coins*; for epigraphy, E. Combe *et al.*, *Répertoire chronologique d'épigraphie arabe*, Paris 1931 f. provides the inscriptions in transcription together with French translations and bibliographical references; for art and architecture, see K. A. C. Cresswell, *Early Muslim Architecture*, and O. Grabar, *The formation of Islamic art*, New Haven, Conn., 1973; for an introduction to the literature on papyrology, see J. Sauvaget's *Introduction to the history of the Muslim East*, based on the second edition as recast by Claude Cahen, Berkeley and Los Angeles 1965, 16–17. This last work is an invaluable guide to resources (primary and secondary) for Islamic history in general, and it should be the first port of call for further information. Chapter 16 is especially relevant for the Umayyads.

Appendix 2

Modern Developments in the Study of and Attitudes to Umayyad History

Although some traditional Muslim scholars, such as the renowned Ibn Khaldun, took a relatively individual view of the Umayyads, in general the hostile attitude to them enshrined in Muslim tradition and summarised in chapter 1 persisted into the nineteenth century. Around the beginning of the twentieth century, however, a reaction against the tradition began and the way was opened for further research. In the works of some European scholars two main developments took place.

One was an advance in understanding the nature of the sources. Insofar as the Umayyads specifically are concerned, the major name was undoubtedly that of the important German Semiticist Julius Wellhausen. Using a method similar to that which he had pioneered in analysing the early books of the Bible, Wellhausen sought to provide a critical analysis of the earlier sources (the so-called *akhbariyyun*) upon which our earliest written sources such as Tabari drew when compiling their accounts of Umayyad history. He thought it was possible to isolate various 'schools', each with its own outlook, special interests and tendencies, among these *akhbariyyun*, and then one could judge their reliability as sources and proceed to write a more accurate account of the period which would correct the distortions inherent in the Muslim tradition.

Slightly earlier, the Hungarian Jewish scholar Ignaz Goldziher had produced the second volume of his *Muhammedanische Studien* (*Muslim Studies* in the English translation) in which he had subjected to critical study the Muslim religious tradition, the mass of reports (*hadiths*) claiming to transmit the words, opinions and deeds of the Prophet Muhammad himself. Goldziher had argued that, far from originating in the time of the Prophet, these *hadiths* emerged mainly in the eighth and ninth centuries and reflect the concerns of Islam as it developed at that time — that is, a century or more after the death of its Prophet. According to Goldziher, a political, religious or legal argument among the Muslims would lead eventually to the elaboration of a *hadith* in which one or more of the conflicting opinions would be supported by attributing it to the Prophet himself. In the course of his discussion Goldziher examined material reflecting the views of supporters and opponents of the Umayyads.

The second development of this period, and one connected with the more critical attitude to Muslim tradition, was a trend to a more positive appreciation of the achievements of the Umayyads. In Wellhausen's work one can see an admiration for the achievements of the Umayyads in creating an empire and holding it together by the development of an effective administrative system, and in the writings of the Belgian Jesuit Henri Lammens this admiration was taken much further. Lammens regarded the Umayyads as the creators of a Syrian-led Arab national state, strong and successful because of their refusal to be dominated by Islam. Matching an expatriate's love of his adopted country (he spent his working life in Lebanon, historically part of greater Syria) with a dislike of Islam, Lammens used his erudite knowledge of the Arabic sources to support an extremely favourable image of Umayyad rule. What he did, in fact, was to accumulate and stress the material in the sources which is favourable to the Umayyads and to use it to attack the general Muslim bias of the tradition.

In general, until relatively recently western scholarship continued and built on these two developments without advancing significantly beyond the works produced by Goldziher, Wellhausen, Lammens and some of their contemporaries like C. H. Becker. In the late 1940s the American D. C. Dennett, who shortly afterwards died in an air accident, argued that Wellhausen's analysis of the Umayyad fiscal system was faulty and that this had implications for his analysis of the so-called 'Abbasid revolution. Another criticism of Wellhausen's interpretation of the overthrow of the Umayyads has come from some scholars who feel that he overstressed the importance of the Persian *mawali* at the expense of the Arabs in the Hashimiyya movement, and there has consequently been a trend to stress the importance of Arabs in the history of the period. In this connection one may mention the works of M. A. Shaban. In spite of these criticisms, however, the structure of Umayyad history created by Wellhausen survived largely intact.

Recently, though, the method of source analysis used by Wellhausen has been criticised as inadequate, or even wrong, so that some scholars would now question whether a detailed history of the period is possible at all. Already by the mid-1950s the general scepticism towards Muslim tradition as a source for the history of early Islam, which Goldziher's work had fostered, had been intensified by the work of his pupil, J. Schacht. By his historical researches into the origins of Muslim law, Schacht claimed to have confirmed and provided detailed evidence for the views of his teacher about the relatively late origin of Muslim tradition and the great influence upon it of, especially, legal disputes. Those who accepted Schacht's findings now had additional ammunition with which to attack the traditional accounts of early Islamic history.

In 1973 A. Noth published his *Quellenkritische Untersuchungen*, in which he attacked the basis of Wellhausen's analysis of the sources. Noth stressed the constant reworking of the historical tradition in the course of its collection and transmission, and emphasised that even the earliest *akhbariyyun*, whose works are excerpted and summarised in our written sources, do not stand at the beginning of the tradition. They too were merely collectors and compilers of material which had already undergone development before it reached them. He argued that it is not possible to get to the origin of the material which has come down to us or to attach the eighth-century *akhbariyyun* to particular 'schools' with clearly defined characteristics, or to describe the bias of a particular scholar. Each of them in fact transmits material reflecting a variety of points of view. Noth then concentrated on isolating the different literary forms and stereotypes within the sources, tending to imply that the sources are little more than a collection of literary *topoi* with a questionable basis in historical reality.

The result is very pessimistic about the possibility of using such sources to reconstruct early Islamic history in detail. It seems that Noth intended his work as an introduction to his own account of the early history of Islam, but in fact the sequel has never appeared.

Other historians have continued to write Umayyad history more or less after the manner of Wellhausen, treating the sources critically but believing that after due criticism it is possible to use them for historical reconstruction. In Germany one may mention Redwan Sayyid and Gernot Rotter as scholars who have attempted to follow the same sort of methods as Wellhausen but to go beyond him by using a wider amount of source material and with the benefit of more modern social and economic concepts. In the United States F. McGraw Donner has produced a history of the Arab conquests and promised a methodological justification for his work. There is no doubt, however, that many now feel inhibitions in this sort of work, and turn instead to source analysis or historiography. Werner Ende and E. L. Petersen come immediately to mind.

One recent major work has attempted to accept the findings of Goldziher, Schacht and Noth and still find a methodology for using the Muslim source material. In her *Slaves on horses* Patricia Crone argued for a biographical or prosopographical approach. Indicating that whenever we can check the basic information given in the Muslim sources (names and dates of caliphs and governors, and so on) by reference to independent sources (for instance, coins, inscriptions, non-Muslim literature) the two usually provide mutual confirmation, she maintained that it is unlikely that all of the information in Muslim sources can be dismissed as later invention or merely literary *topoi*. Such apparently incidental details as those regarding an individual's status and tribal or factional alignment, his marriage ties and his social or political links, are likely to be based on reality, and it is this sort of information, rather than, for example, the accounts of the motives of rebels or caliphs engaged in the major events, which the historian should concentrate on. From this point of view the cohesiveness of Dr Crone's book is as impressive as its conceptual sophistication. A consequence of this approach, and one which has been anticipated or shared by others, is a movement away from the straightforward narrative of political events towards a greater interest in institutions, social and religious history. M. G. Morony's work is another example of this trend.

In the modern Islamic, and especially Arab, world Umayyad history has sometimes served as a mirror reflecting current political and religious preoccupations. This does not mean that all modern Arab or Muslim writing on the period should be read as a comment on current affairs or that one can forecast what a particular writer will say if one knows his religious or political position first. But since the Umayyad period was crucial for the arabisation and islamisation of the Middle East, it is obvious that Arabs or Muslims pondering their identity in the modern world will find much food for thought in the history of the dynasty.

In particular, the possible tension between Islam and Arab nationalism could affect views of the Umayyads. From the Arab nationalist perspective the dynasty could be seen as one of potential culture heroes in view of its role in the creation of the first great Arab empire, but Muslim tradition, as we have seen, presents a generally hostile picture of the Umayyads and this could lead to problems if one stresses the Muslim, rather than Arab, character of one's own identity. This general and perhaps only latent tension might then become sharper and more real if, on the one hand, one holds a specifically Shi'ite interpretation of Muslim history, since the Shi'ite tradition is more hostile than the Sunni towards the Umayyads, or, on the other hand, one holds to a Syrian rather than general Arab form of nationalism.

It was in the years before the Second World War that debate about the role of the Umayyads and their place in Arab and Islamic history became particularly intense. Interestingly, support for the dynasty came from a reform movement within Sunni Islam known as the Salafiyya, and not merely from the partisans of Arab or Syrian nationalism. Probably the Salafiyya was influenced by the same concern for continuity within Sunni Islam and the same awareness of the position of Mu'awiya and the other Umayyads in the polemic between Sunnis and Shi'ites as had moderated the anti-Umayyad trend in earlier Muslim tradition.

The proponents of the Umayyads used some of the same arguments as the European scholars: insistence on a proper understanding of the religious outlook inherent in the source material, awareness of the need to understand the difficult historical circumstances in which the Umayyads found themselves, and selection and emphasis of the material favourable to them in Muslim tradition.

Potential for hostility between Sunnis and Shi'ites on the issue was particularly strong in Iraq where a large Shi'ite community has from time to time felt itself oppressed by the Sunnis in whose hands political power has tended to remain. Already in the 1920s there were public disturbances when it was felt that the Sunnis, anxious to promote the ideals of Arab nationalism, fostered too favourable an attitude to the Umayyads in the material used in schools.

Since the Second World War the issue has, perhaps, not been so prominent, but it is easy to see a number of ways in which Umayyad history can be made to relate to contemporary issues. The problem of Israel and Palestine, for example, has fostered an interest in Umayyad policies in the region and especially in the importance of Jerusalem for the Umayyads. Again, hostility between Iraq and Syria may be behind some of the more negative judgments on the

Umayyads made by some Iraqis, aware that the sources tend to portray Umayyad rule as Syrian domination over the Muslim centres of Iraq.

The question of modern Arab and Muslim attitudes to the Umayyads has been studied in detail by Werner Ende in his *Arabische Nation und islamische Geschichte*.

Bibliography

Abel, A., 'Le khalife, presence sacrée', *SI*, 7 (1957)

Barthold, W., 'The caliph 'Umar II and the contradictory information about his personality', *IQ*, 15 (1971)

Becker, C. H., 'The expansion of the Saracens' in *CMedH*, ii, Cambridge 1913. German version: 'Die Ausbreitung der Araber im Mittelmeergebiet' in his *Islamstudien*, i, Leipzig, 1924

——, 'Studien zur Omajjadengeschichte. a) 'Omar II', *ZA*, 15 (1900)

Beeston, A. F. L. *et al.* (ed.), *Arab literature to the end of the Umayyad period*, Cambridge, 1983

Beg, M. A. J., 'Mu'āwiya: a critical survey', *IC*, 51 (1977)

Bell, H. I., 'The administration of Egypt under the Umayyad caliphs', *BZ*, 28 (1928)

Blachère, R., 'Le prince omayyade al-Walīd (II) ibn Yazīd et son rôle littéraire' in *Mélanges Gaudefroy-Demombynes*, Cairo, 1935

Blau, J., *The emergence and linguistic background of Judaeo-Arabic*, London, 1965

Bosworth, C. E., *Sīstān under the Arabs*, Rome, 1968

——, 'Rajā' b. Ḥaywa al-Kindī and the Umayyad caliphs', *IQ*, 16 (1972)

——, ''Ubaidallāh b. Abī Bakra and the "Army of Destruction" in Zābulistān', *Isl.* (1973)

——, *Al-Maqrīzī's 'Book of contention and strife concerning the relations between the Banū Umayya and the Banū Hāshim'*, Manchester, 1980

——, 'The coming of Islam to Afghanistan' in *Islam in Asia, i, South Asia*, ed. Y. Friedmann, Jerusalem, 1984

Bravmann, M. M., '*Sunnah* and related concepts' in his *The spiritual background of early Islam*, Leiden, 1972

Brett, M., 'The islamisation of North Africa' in *idem* (ed.), *Islam and modernisation in North Africa*, London, 1973

Brock, S. P., 'Syriac sources for seventh century history' in *Byzantine and modern Greek studies*, ii (1976)

Brünnow, R., *Die Charidschiten unter den ersten Umayyeden*, Leiden, 1884

Buhl, F., 'Die Krisis der Umajjadenherrschaft im Jahre 684', *ZA*, 27 (1912)

Bulliet, R., *Conversion to Islam in the medieval period*, Cambridge Mass., 1979

Cahen, C., 'Points de vue sur la revolution 'abbaside', *RH*, 230 (1963)

Canard, M., 'Les expeditions des Arabes contre Constantinople', *JA*, 108 (1926)

Caskel, W., *Der Felsendom und die Wallfahrt nach Jerusalem*, Cologne and Opladen, 1963

Cook, M. A., *Early Muslim dogma*, Cambridge, 1981
Coulson, N. J., *A history of Islamic law*, Edinburgh, 1964
Cresswell, K. A. C., *A short account of early Muslim architecture*, London, 1958
——, *Early Muslim architecture*, 2nd edn, Oxford, 1969
Crone, P., *Slaves on horses*, Cambridge, 1980
——, 'Islam, Júdeo-Christianity and Byzantine iconoclasm', *JSAI*, 1 (1980)
Crone, P. and Cook, M. A., *Hagarism*, Cambridge, 1977
Dennett, D., *Conversion and the poll-tax in early Islam*, Cambridge Mass., 1950
——, *Marwān b. Muḥammad; the passing of the Umayyad caliphate*, PhD thesis, Harvard University, 1939
Derenk, D., *Leben und Dichtung des Omaiyadenkalifen al-Walīd ibn Yazīd*, Freiburg im Breisgau, 1974
Dixon, A. A., *The Umayyad caliphate 65–86/684–705*, London, 1971
Djait, H., 'Les Yamanites à Kufa au 1er siècle de l'hégire', *JESHO*, 1976
Donner, F. McGraw, *The early Islamic conquests*, Princeton, 1981
Dunlop, D. M., *The history of the Jewish Khazars*, Princeton, 1954
Duri, 'Abd al-'Azīz, 'Ḍaw' jadīd 'ala 'l-da'wa al-'abbāsiyya', in *Majallat Kulliyat al-ādāb*, ii, Baghdad, 1957
——, *The rise of historical writing among the Arabs*, English trans., Princeton, 1983
Encyclopaedia of Islam, 1st edition, 4 vols. and Supplement, Leiden 1913–42; 2nd edition in progress, Leiden 1954-
Ende, W., *Arabische Nation und islamische Geschichte. Die Umayyaden im Urteil arabischer Autoren des 20 Jahrhunderts*, Beirut, 1977
Fariq, K. A., 'A remarkable early Muslim governor, Ziyād b. Abīh', *IC*, 26 (1952)
——, *Ziyād b. Abīh*, London, 1966
——, 'The story of an Arab diplomat', *Studies in Islam*, 3 (1966) and 4 (1967)
Faris, N. A., 'Development in Arab historiography as reflected in the struggle between 'Alī and Mu'āwiya', in *Historians of the Middle East*, ed. P. M. Holt and B. Lewis, London, 1962
Forand, P., 'The status of the land and the inhabitants of the sawad during the first two centuries of Islam', *JESHO*, 14 (1971)
Friedmann, Y., 'A contribution to the early history of Islam in India' in *Studies in memory of Gaston Wiet*, ed. M. Rosen-Ayalon, Jerusalem, 1977
——, 'The origins and significance of the Chach Nama' in *Islam in Asia*, i, South Asia, ed. Y. Friedmann, Jerusalem, 1984
Frye, R. N., 'The 'Abbasid conspiracy and modern revolutionary theory', *Indo-Iranica*, 5 (1952)
——, 'The rôle of Abu Muslim in the 'Abbāsid revolution', *MW*, 37 (1947)
—— (ed.), *The Cambridge History of Iran*, vol. iv, London, 1975
Gabrieli, F., *Il califfato di Hishâm*, Alexandria, 1935
——, 'Al Walīd b. Yazīd, il califfo e il poeta', *RSO*, 15 (1935)
——, 'La rivolta dei Muhallabiti e il nuovo Baladuri nel Iraq', *Rend. Linc.*, series vi, vol. 14 (1938)

——, *Muhammad and the conquests of Islam*, London, 1968
——, 'Muḥammad b. Qāsim al-Thaqafī and the Arab conquest of Sind', *East and West*, 15 (1964–5)
Gelder, H. D. von, *Muhtar de valsche Profeet*, Leiden, 1888
Gibb, H. A. R., *The Arab conquests in central Asia*, London, 1923
——, 'The fiscal rescript of 'Umar II', *Arabica*, 2 (1955)
——, *Studies on the civilisation of Islam*, London, 1962
Goitein, S. D., 'The historical background of the erection of the Dome of the Rock', *JAOS*, 70 (1950)
——, 'The sanctity of Jerusalem and Palestine in early Islam' in his *Studies in Islamic history and institutions*, Leiden, 1966
Goldziher, I., *Muhammedanische Studien*, 2 vols., Halle, 1889–90; English trans. *Muslim Studies*, 2 vols., London, 1967–71
——, 'Du sens propre des expressions Ombre de Dieu, etc.', *RHR*, 35 (1897)
——, 'Mu'āwiya I, der Begründer des Islamstaates', *Deutsche Literatur-zeitung*, 30 (1909)
——, *Gesammelte Schriften*, ed. J. Desomogyi, Hildesheim, 1967
Grabar, O., 'The Umayyad Dome of the Rock in Jerusalem', *Ars Orientalis*, 3 (1959)
——, 'Al-Mushatta, Baghdad and Wasit' in *The world of Islam. Studies in honour of Philip K. Hitti*, London, 1959
——, 'Notes sur les ceremonies umayyades' in *Studies in memory of Gaston Wiet*, ed. M. Rosen-Ayalon, Jerusalem, 1977
Grierson, P., 'The monetary reforms of 'Abd al-Malik', *JESHO*, 3 (1960)
Grunebaum, G. E. von, *Medieval Islam*, Chicago, 1948
——, *Muslim festivals*, New York, 1951
Habib, I., 'A study of Ḥajjāj bin Yusuf's outlook and policies in the light of the Chach Nāma', *Bulletin of the Institute of Islamic Studies*, 6–7 (1962–3)
Hawting, G. R., 'The Umayyads and ᵗʰᵉ Hijāz', *Proceedings of the 5th Seminar for Arabian Studies*, London, 1972
——, 'The significance of the slogan lā ḥukma illā li'llāh, etc.', *BSOAS*, 41 (1978)
Hinds, M., 'Kufan political alignments and their background in the mid-seventh century A.D.', *IJMES*, 1971
——, 'The banners and battle cries of the Arabs at Ṣiffīn', *Al-Abḥāth*, 1971
——, 'The murder of the caliph 'Uthmān', *IJMES*, 1972
Hirschberg, J. W., 'The sources of Muslim traditions concerning Jerusalem', *RO*, 1953
Hitti, P. K., *History of Syria*, London, 1951
Hodgson, M. G., 'How did the early Shī'a become sectarian?', *JAOS*, 75 (1955)
——, *The venture of Islam*, i, Chicago, 1974
Ibn Isḥāq, *Sīra* (redaction of Ibn Hisham), English trans., A. Guillaume, *The life of Muhammad*, London, 1955
Jafri, S. M., *Origins and early development of Shi'a Islam*, London, 1979
Jāḥiẓ, al-, *Risāla fi'l B. Umayya* (=*Risāla fi'l-Nābita*), French trans., C. Pellat in *AIEOr. (Alger)*, 1952

Jeffery, A., 'Ghevond's text of the correspondence between 'Umar II and Leo III', *Harvard Theological Review*, 1944

Jenkins, R. J. H., 'Cyprus between Byzantium and Islam', in *Studies presented to D. M. Robinson*, London, 1953

Jones, A. H. M., *The later Roman Empire*, Oxford, 1973

Juynboll, G. H. A., 'The *qurrā'* in early Islamic history', *JESHO*, 16 (1973)

——, 'The date of the great *fitna'*, *Arabica*, 20 (1973)

—— (ed.), *Studies on the first century of Islamic society*, Southern Illinois University Press, 1982

Kennedy, H., *The early Abbasid caliphate*, London, 1981

Kessler, C., "Abd al-Malik's inscription in the Dome of the Rock: a reconsideration', *JRAS* (1970)

Kister, M. J., 'The battle of the Harra', in *Studies in memory of Gaston Wiet*, ed. M. Rosen-Ayalon, Jerusalem, 1977

Kohlberg, E., 'Some Imāmī Shī'ī interpretations of Umayyad history' in *Studies on the first century of Islamic society*, ed. G. H. A. Juynboll, Southern Illinois Univ. Press, 1982

Lammens, H., *Etudes sur le règne du calife omaiyade Mo'âwia 1er*, Paris, 1908

——, *Le Califat de Yazîd 1er*, Beirut, 1910–21

——, 'Mo'âwia II ou le dernier des Sofianides', *RSO*, 7 (1916–18)

——, *Etudes sur le siècle des Omayyades*, Beirut, 1930

Lapidus, I. M., 'The conversion of Egypt to Islam', *IOS*, 1972

Levtzion, N. (ed.), *Conversion to Islam*, London, 1979

Lewis, B., *The Arabs in History*, London, 1956

——, and Holt, P. M. (eds.), *Historians of the Middle East*, London, 1962

Mackensen, R. S., 'Arabic books and libraries in the Umayyad period', *AJSL*, 52 (1936), 53 (1937) and 54 (1937)

Madelung, W., "Abd Allāh b. al-Zubayr and the Mahdi', *JNES*, 40 (1981)

Maqrīzī, al-, *Al-Nizā' fa'l-takhāsum fīmā bayna B. Umayya wa-B. Hāshim*, English trans. C. E. Bosworth, *Maqrīzī's 'Book of contention and strife . . .'*, Manchester, 1980

Massignon, L., 'Explication du plan de Kufa', *Mélanges Maspero*, Cairo, 1934–40

——, 'Explication du plan de Basra', *Westöstliche Abhandlungen R. Tschudi*, ed. F. Meier, Wiesbaden, 1954

Mones, H., 'The Umayyads of the east and west', *Der Orient in der Forschung. Festschrift für O. Spies*, ed. W. Hoenerbach, Wiesbaden, 1967

Morony, M. G., *Iraq after the Muslim conquest*, Princeton, 1984

——, 'Religious communities in late Sasanian and early Muslim Iraq', *JESHO*, 1974

——, 'The effects of the Muslim conquest on the Persian population of Iraq', *Iran*, 1976

Moscati, S., 'Le massacre des Umayyades dans l'histoire et dans les fragments poétiques', *Archiv Orientální*, 1950

——, 'Il testamento di Abu Hašim', *RSO*, 27 (1952)

——, 'Per una storia dell' antica ší'a, *RSO*, 30 (1955)

Nagel, T., *Untersuchungen zur Entstehung des abbasidischen Kalifates*,

Bonn, 1972

Nöldeke, T., 'Zur Geschichte der Omaijaden', *ZDMG*, 55 (1901)

Noth, A., *Quellenkritische Studien zu Themen, Formen und Tendenzen frühislamischer Geschichtsüberlieferung*, Bonn, 1973

——, 'Zum Verhältnis von kalifaler Zentralgewalt und Provinzen in umayyadischer Zeit: die 'Ṣulḥ-'Anwa' Traditionen für Agypten und Iraq', *WI*, 14 (1973)

Omar, F., *The 'Abbasid caliphate 132/750–170/786*, Baghdad, 1969

——, 'The composition of 'Abbasid support', *Bulletin of the College of Arts, Baghdad*, ii (1968)

Pellat, C., *Le milieu basrien et la formation de Gāḥiẓ*, Paris, 1953

Perier, J., *Vie d' al-Ḥadjdjâdj ibn Yousuf*, Paris, 1904

Petersen, E. L., *'Alī and Mu'āwiya in early Arabic tradition*, Copenhagen, 1964

Poliak, A., 'L'arabisation de l'orient semitique', *REI*, 12 (1938)

Quatremère, E., 'Mémoire historique sur la vie d'Abd-allah ben-Zobair', *JA*, series 2, nos. 9 and 10

Rizzitano, U., "Abdalaziz b. Marwān governatore d'Egitto', *Rend. Linc.*, series 8, 2 (1941)

Rotter, G., 'Abu Zur'a al-Dimašqi (st. 281/894) und das Problem der frühen arabischen Geschichtsschreibung in Syrien', *Die Welt des Orients*, 1970–1

——, *Die Umayyaden und der zweite Bürgerkrieg (688–692)*, Wiesbaden, 1982

Rubinacci, R., 'Il califfo 'Abd al-Malik b. Marwan e gli ibāḍiti', *AIUON*, new series, 5 (1953)

Salibi, K., *Syria under Islam*, New York, 1977

Sauvaget, J., *La mosquée omeyyade de Medine*, Paris, 1947

Sayed, R., *Die Revolte des Ibn al-As'at und die Koranlesser*, Freiburg, 1977

Schacht, J., *Introduction to Islamic law*, Oxford, 1964

Sellheim, R., *Der zweite Bürgerkrieg in Islam*, Wiesbaden, 1970

Serjeant, R. B., 'The *sunnah jāmi'ah*: pacts with the Yathrib Jews and the *taḥrīm* of Yathrib', *BSOAS*, 41 (1978)

Shaban, M. A., *The 'Abbasid revolution*, Cambridge, 1970

——, *Islamic history. A new interpretation. I. AD 600–750 (AH 132)*, Cambridge, 1971

Sharon, M., 'The 'Abbasid da'wa reexamined on the basis of the discovery of a new source' in *Arabic and Islamic Studies*, ed. J. Mansour, Ramat Gan, 1973

——, *Black banners from the east. The establishment of the 'Abbasid state — Incubation of a revolt*, Jerusalem, 1983

——, 'An Arabic inscription from the time of 'Abd al-Malik', *BSOAS*, 29 (1966)

Siddiqi, A. H., 'Insignia of sovereignty during the Umayyad caliphate', *PPHS*, 3 (1953)

——, 'A paper on the character of the Umayyad caliphate', *PPHS*, 8 (1958)

Sprengling, M., 'Persian into Arabic', *AJSL*, 1939 and 1940

Thomson, W., 'Kharijitism and the Kharijites', *MacDonald Presentation Volume*, Princeton, 1933

——, 'The character of early Islamic sects', *Ignace Goldziher Memorial Volume*, Budapest, 1948

Tucker, W., 'Rebels and gnostics: al-Muġira Ibn Saʻid and the Muġiriyya', *Arabica*, 22 (1975)

——, 'Bayān b. Samʻān and the Bayāniyya: Shiʻite extremists of Umayyad Iraq', *MW*, 65 (1975)

——, 'Abū Manṣūr al-ʻIjlī and the Manṣūriyya: a study in medieval terrorism', *Isl.*, 1977

——, "Abd Allāh b. Muʻāwiya and the Janāḥiyya: rebels and ideologues of the late Umayyad period', *SI*, 51 (1980)

Van Ess, J., 'Les Qadarites et la Ġailaniyya de Yazid III', *SI*, 41 (1970)

Van Vloten, G., *Recherches sur la domination arabe, le Chiitisme, et les croyances messianiques sous le Khalifat des Umaiyades*, Amsterdam, 1894

Veccia Vaglieri, L., 'Il conflitto ʻAli-Muʼawiya e la seccessione kharigita riesaminati alla luce di fonte ibadite', *AIUON*, 4 (1951)

Walker, J.A., *A catalogue of the Arab-Byzantine and post-reform Umaiyad coins*, London, 1956

Watt, W. M., *Muḥammad at Mecca*, London, 1953

——, *Muḥammad at Medina*, London, 1956

——, 'Shiʻism under the Umayyads', *JRAS* (1960)

——, 'Khārijite thought in the Umayyad period', *Isl.*, 36 (1961)

——, 'God's Caliph. Qurʼanic interpretations and Umayyad claims', *Iran and Islam*, ed. C. E. Bosworth, Edinburgh, 1971

——, *The formative period of Islamic thought*, Edinburgh, 1973

Wellhausen, J., 'Die Kämpfe der Araber mit den Romäern in der Zeit der Umaijaden', *Nachrichten der königlichen Gesellschaft des Wissenschaften*, Göttingen, 1901

——, *Die religiös-politischen Oppositionsparteien im alten Islam*, Berlin 1901; Eng. tr., *The religio-political factions in early Islam*, Amsterdam, 1975

——, *Das arabische Reich und sein Sturz*, Berlin 1902; Eng. tr., *The Arab kingdom and its fall*, Calcutta, 1927

Wüstenfeld, F., *Die Familie el-Zubeir. Der Tod Muçʻab ben el-Zubeir aus den Muwaffakîyât des Abu Abdallah el-Dimaschkî*, Göttingen, 1878

Index

This index is arranged word by word according to the order of the Roman alphabet. In the ordering, no account is taken of the symbols ' or ' for the Arabic letters 'ayn and hamza, or of the Arabic definite article al ('l).